THE EVERYDAY
SOUS VIDE COOKBOOK

Jamie Stewart

Warning-Disclaimer

The purpose of this book is to educate and entertain. The author or publisher does not guarantee that anyone following the techniques, suggestions, tips, ideas, or strategies will become successful. The author and publisher shall have neither liability or responsibility to anyone with respect to any loss or damage caused, or alleged to be caused, directly or indirectly by the information contained in this book.

CONTENTS

INTRODUCTION

Sous vide technique celebrates the beauty of modern cooking, helping you make an intensely flavored food and eat healthier. It allows you to take a moment of inspiration and create your culinary chef-d'oeuvre (from French chef-d'oeuvre – a masterpiece) in your own kitchen.

It's no surprise that sous vide cooking method is rapidly becoming one of the most popular culinary techniques all over the world. This is the secret weapon of world's top chefs. If you can't cook like a famous chef, you can at least learn some advanced techniques that you can implement in your kitchen immediately and achieve authentic results.

A Quick Start Guide to Sous Vide Cooking

Even though top chefs have used the sous vide cooking method for decades, sous vide has just recently found its place in the home kitchen. Most people enjoy chef-inspired meals but they quickly become discouraged when they discover that they require culinary skills, time and effort. Luckily, sous vide cooking method is an incredible way to save time and money, including a maximum taste and minimal cleanup. Ultimately, cooking at home brings a family together and every gathering becomes a special event!

Regardless of the simplicity of sous vide cooking, there are a lot of tips and tricks to bear in mind that can help you to achieve the best result. Here are some of our most frequently asked questions about the Sous Vide cooking method.

1. What Is Sous Vide Cooking?

Sous vide (French for "under vacuum") is a method of cooking in which your food is sealed in a food-grade cooking pouch and cooked in a preheated water bath, at the temperature specified in the recipe.

Simply put, sous vide is the method of cooking at a strictly controlled temperature – just hot enough to cook your food to perfect doneness; as a matter of fact, your food should be cooked at the temperature it will be served at. For example, if you are cooking your fish to medium, you want to serve it at 140 degrees F. This method takes some time, up to several hours, but the entire piece will be cooked to that perfect state of "just right".

And ultimately, your food is cooked to your liking every time. Whether your preference is a flaky, tender fish, butter-soft pork chops or crispy, fork-tender potatoes, you can rely on the sous vide cooking method.

2. WHY SOUS VIDE?

You don't have to be a culinary expert to make the best sous vide recipes. On the contrary, it's pretty simple, hands-off cooking that everyone can master. At first glance, it may seem difficult for an average cook. Don't be misled by the French name. The name may sound fancy, but cooking sous vide is easier than you think. Simply throw all ingredients into a cooking pouch and vacuum seal it; then, set your cooker, submerge the pouch in the preheated water bath and sit back. The beauty of this cooking method is that it allows you to cook several meals simultaneously. It results in all-star dishes that cannot be achieved by other traditional cooking methods. It couldn't be better, right?!

3. EXPLORING THE SCIENCE OF COOKING.

Unlike other cooking methods, sous vide allows you to have control over heat, temperature, and cooking time. There are a few major points you need to know to get started.

As you probably already know, heat is one of the most important things in cooking. It can transform your food into the real piece of art or into something dull and over- or undercooked. A sous vide bag protects your food from direct contact with water and "transfers" the desired heat straight to your food. In other words, it is cooking with precision. The sous vide technique enables you to effectively set exact temperatures, depending on what you are trying to accomplish.

Almost every kind of meat begins to lose its weight and moisture above 140 degrees F as the high temperature causes the collagen in the animal tissue to shrink. Using sous vide allows you to tenderize any cuts of meat without causing it to lose its flavor, texture and moisture.

The other considerably important component is – the cooking time! Because the entire process takes place at low temperatures (up to a maximum of 185 degrees F) we should increase the cooking time. It's good to know this, even if you are not a scientist.

Take pork chops as an example. If you prefer tender and very juicy chops, the ideal temperature is 130 degrees F. However, if you like firm pork chops, you should set your cooker to 150 degrees F. And finally, if you prefer well-done and little dry pork, you should use 160 degrees F. The timing range is the same – 1 to 4 hours in all three cases. Actually, everything is grounded in logic, this is the science of good cooking!

4. What Could You Achieve?

An easy idea for effortless cooking – If you don't like the idea of going grocery shopping, washing, chopping, stirring, peeling, cooking and cleaning up, give the sous vide technique a try. Basically, there are four simple steps: 1) season your food; 2) set your device 3) throw the ingredients into a cooking pouch and transfer it to the preheated water bath; 4) finally, pour a glass of wine and let your reliable "kitchen companion" do the rest. And soon you will see – it's impossible to ruin your meal!

Cash-saving meals to feed the whole family – Yes, you will be able to save your hard-earned money with the sous vide method. It may seem expensive at first, but you will make a good long-term investment.

The sous vide cooking appliance is designed to make the most of budget-friendly ingredients such as root vegetables, cheap cuts of meat, frozen fruits, whole chicken or turkey, etc. You can purchase tougher meats but your sous vide cooker will transform them into moist, tender, finger-licking pieces of meat. This way, you can cook your meals in bulk and provide your family with valuable nutrition during the upcoming days. Many of the sous vide recipes call for staples you already have in your pantry.

Even though sous vide results in professional-quality dishes, you don't need an expensive professional device. There are a lot of affordable machines on the market that could be just good enough. Even the most affordable sous vide devices work with a water bath of 5 to 6 gallons (i.e. 20 l); it should be enough for home use. As a matter of fact, you can cook a few different types of food at the same time. Just throw each type of food into a separate cooking pouch. Also, cooking for the whole family has never been easier than with the sous vide setup!

Get ahead – You can cook almost every kind of sous vide meal, and then, transfer the pouch to an ice-water bath and let it cool completely. Finally, place it in your refrigerator until ready to use again. You can also slice your meals easily and save space in your freezer. When you are ready to eat, simply defrost your food; after that, you can reheat and finish the food on the grill, in a skillet, or in your oven. Afterward, place the sauce or salad on your food, serve, and enjoy! Be inspired by this revolutionary cooking method and delight your guests with flavorful, fancy meals, regardless of your skill level. Throwing a dinner party has never been so easy!

Hassle-Free Cooking Your Grandma Would Love

With all that in mind, it's time to use this inspiring technology to make sous vide recipes.

1. Cooking vegetable and fruits sous vide.

Sous vide allows you to cook your veggies and fruits at the desired temperature so there is less risk of under- or overcooking them. Hence, it is not surprising that the sous vide method has caught fire around the world!

You can make everything, from easy appetizers to gourmet vegan main courses and holiday desserts! Sous vide allows your veggies to tenderize without losing their nutrients and texture. It all boils down to an appropriate temperature and the right cooking time. Further, it depends on your personal preferences. Take potatoes as an example. If you are always looking for the perfect way to make boiled potatoes, enjoy this low-and-slow cooking experience. Set your cooker to 183 degrees F (this is the recommended temperature for most fruits and vegetables) and throw the potatoes into the vacuum seal bags; it results in fork-tender potato bites that retain the maximum amount of their valuable nutrients. This super simple method will help you make the best French fries, aromatic Mediterranean potatoes or the easiest roasted potatoes ever, fresh and flavorsome salads and other potato recipes.

You don't have to eat a raw diet to stay healthy and fit. You just need to choose the best cooking methods to preserve valuable nutrients from your whole foods.

As you probably already know, water-soluble vitamins, especially most of the B vitamins and vitamin C, are easily dissolved and washed away by water. On the other hand, Vitamins A, D and E are fat-soluble. Instead, you should use the sous vide method to avoid destroying any vitamins – nutrients do not evaporate into thin air because they can't escape from the sealed environment. Give sous vide a try and take the extra step towards healthy eating!

2. COOKING MEAT SOUS VIDE.

When it comes to meat and poultry, everything depends on the type of meat you use as well as the desired taste and appearance. It is well known that cooking methods that utilize small amounts of water and cooking oil, and don't require high temperatures preserve valuable nutrients best.

Sous vide cooking is the best way to produce juicy and tender meat, especially if you cook less tender cuts. When you're cooking sous vide, you achieve more consistent results regardless of which part of an animal you use. Sous vide can tenderize any kind of meat and turn tough fibers into gelatin so it is much easier for our stomach to digest. It's about predictable results, even the cheapest cuts of meat turn out good, without exceptions. Besides all that, it never hurts to marinate your meat before cooking.

Cooking temperature is a key to success, but, as we said before, cooking time matters a lot. How to select the right temperature? The amount of time will depend on the type of meat, as well as the thickness or tenderness of the meat in the cooking bag. For instance, if you tend to cook the whole chicken for your Sunday family lunch, you should separate dark meat (chicken legs and thighs) from white meat (breasts). Then, place each type of meat in a separate cooking pouch. Here's the thing: dark meat requires higher temperature (165-175 degrees F) and more time (6-8 hours), while white meat requires "gentle" cooking and less time to cook. Yes, of course, you can use other methods such as roasting, searing, grilling and so forth. But, with sous vide, every part of your bird will be cooked at their perfect temperature, from edge to center, without any loss of structure or flavor.

The same goes for turkey, pork, beef, etc. Doubtless, there is a big difference when cooking back ribs, brisket or bottom round London broil.

Here are a few more tricks you should always keep up your sleeve:

> ➢ Salt and pepper your meat before vacuum sealing to enhance the flavors of your meal. Make sure to use high-quality salt.

> ➢ In addition, the right balance of seasoning can yield a huge flavor boost in a sealed environment, so be careful. It's better to use dried powders instead of fresh herbs, too.

> ➢ To make deli-style dishes, try to smoke the meat before placing it in the bag. If you are in a hurry, you can just add a few dashes of liquid smoke.

3. COOKING FROZEN FOOD SOUS VIDE.

This is one of the greatest advantages of sous vide cooking. You can buy your food in bulk and keep it in your freezer until ready to use. Unlike other cooking methods, you don't have to thaw meat first when you are cooking sous vide. Just place the frozen food in the cooking pouch and submerge the pouch in the preheated water bath. Moreover, you can cook food directly in its own packaging simply because many products come vacuum sealed already.

The main question is: "How long should I cook frozen foods with sous vide? Follow the recommended time for cooking fresh food; now, divide that time by two and add that number to the cooking time for fresh food. The formula is $X + (X/2) = Y$.

Tips for Using This Recipe Collection – Cook like Michelin-Starred Chefs!

If you're just getting started with Sous vide cooking, check out these 150 recipes. At the very beginning, select the recipes that best suit your taste and your culinary skills. Later, the more you cook with sous vide cooker, the more you will learn about this fantastic technique and get used to the best homemade meals.

To make sous vide cooking super-easy, each and every recipe includes the ingredient list, detailed step-by-step directions, the number of servings and cooking time. The recipes include the nutritional information that will help you to stick to your diet goals. In addition, you will find many creative ideas to make your meals better, "secret" kitchen tips, food facts you always wanted to know, and so forth. This recipe collection illustrates the power of slow cooking in a temperature-controlled environment, which will help you become a cook that you never knew you could be! As a matter of fact, the beauty of this revolutionary technique is that it does more than just cook perfect meat. It is a great way to cook a variety of comfort foods, pasteurize eggs, make homemade yogurt, and infuse booze for the best cocktails ever!

Cooking at home is easier than you can imagine and it is also healthier and cheaper. If you're new to sous vide and wondering where to start, this recipe collection contains the answers. In addition to being unique and delicious, these recipes promote a well-balanced diet for life-long health as well as home cooking which is always a good idea. The recipes in this collection call for good fats, fresh vegetables, good animal protein, less fat, and so forth. They are organized into nine main chapters: Vegetables & Fruits; Chicken; Turkey & Duck; Pork; Beef; Fish & Seafood; Vegan; Snacks & Appetizers; and Desserts.

Remember: "The doctor of the future will no longer treat the human frame with drugs, but rather will cure and prevent disease with nutrition." ~ Thomas Edison.

By all means, with sous vide, you will find the inspiration to cook like a 3-star chef and eat much better!

Sous Vide Recommended Times and Temperatures

POULTRY	THICKNESS (inch)	TEMPERATURE (F)	TIME
Chicken breast, bone in	2	146 or higher	2.5-6 hours
Chicken breast, Boneless	1	146 or higher	1-4 hours
Duck breast	1	134 or higher	90 min-6 hours
Turkey breast, bone in	2.75	146 or higher	4-8 hours
Turkey breast, boneless	2	146 or higher	2.5-6 hours
Chicken leg and thigh, bone in		165-176	4-8 hours
Chicken thigh, boneless	1	165-176	2-6 hours
Duck drumstick		165-176	8-18 hours
Split game hen	2.75	150 or higher	6-8 hours
Turkey leg or thigh		165-176	8-10 hours
PORK			
Baby back ribs		165	4-24 hours
Belly (quick)	2	185	5-8 hours
Belly (slow)	2	167	24-72 hours
Chops and cutlets	1	134 or higher	2-8 hours
Chops and cutlets	2	134 or higher	4-10 hours
Spare ribs	2.75	160-176	12-30 hours
Tenderloin	1.5	134 or higher	90 min-8 hours

BEEF, GAME, LAMB, VEAL			
Chops, cutlets, tenderloin, rib-eye, T-bone	1	134 or higher	1-4 hours
Chops, cutlets, tenderloin, rib-eye, T-bone	2	134 or higher	3-6 hours
Game	1	134 or higher	10-24 hours
Lamb roast and leg	2.75	134 or higher	10-48 hours
Rank steak and brisket	1	134 or higher	8-24 hours
Rank steak and brisket	2	134 or higher	12-30 hours
Spare ribs	2	134 or higher	24-72 hours
SEAFOOD	THICKNESS (inch)	TEMPERATURE (F)	TIME
FISH Snapper, Tuna, Halibut, Salmon, Trout, Mackerel, Sole	0.5-1	126 or higher	20-30 min
FISH Snapper, Tuna, Halibut, Salmon, Trout, Mackerel, Sole	1-2	126 or higher	30-40 min
Lobster	1	140	45-60 min
Scallops	1	140	40-60 min
Shrimp	jumbo	140	30-40 min
VEGETABLES			
ROOT Carrots, Potato, Turnips, Beets, Parsnips, Celery root	1	183	1-4 hours
ROOT Carrots, Potato, Turnips, Beets, Parsnips, Celery root	1-2	183	2.5-4 hours
TENDER Asparagus, Broccoli, Corn, Cauliflower, Eggplant, Fennel, Green Beans, Onions, Peas Squash	1	183	30 min-1.5 hours

FRUIT			
FIRM Apple and pear	1	183	45 min–2 hours
SOFT Peach, Apricot, Plum, Mango, Papaya, Nectarine, Berries	1	183	30 min-1 hour
EGGS			
Soft-cooked in shell, quick	large	167	15-18 min
Soft-cooked in shell, slow	large	146	45 min-1.5 hours
Hard-cooked in shell	large	160	45 min-1.5 hours
Pasteurized in shell	large	135	1.25-2 hours
Scrambled (5 eggs)	large	167	20 min

Doneness Target Temperatures

FOOD	DONENESS	TEMPERATURE
Eggs	soft cooked	146-167
	hard cooked	160
	scrambled	167
	pasteurized	135
Vegetables and fruits	–	183-190
Beef, Game, Veal, Lamb	rare	120
	medium rare	134
	medium	140
	medium well	150
	well done	160 and higher
Pork	medium rare	134
	medium	140
	well done	160 and higher
Poultry	medium	140-146
	medium rare	134
	well done	176
Fish and seafood	rare	116
	medium rare	126
	medium	140

VEGETABLES AND FRUITS

1. Saucy Sweet Potatoes with Zucchini and Peppers

 4 Servings

 Ready in about 20 minutes

PER SERVING:
225 Calories; 12.9g Fat;
27.3g Carbs; 2.8g Protein;
8.8g Sugars

Crisp seared Brussels sprouts are yummy on their own. You can serve them with a little dipping sauce if desired.

Ingredients

- 3/4 pound Brussels sprouts, trimmed and quartered
- 4 tablespoons olive oil
- 1 tablespoon oyster sauce
- 1 teaspoon brown sugar

- 1/3 teaspoon sea salt flakes
- 1/4 teaspoon ground black pepper
- 1/2 teaspoon red pepper flakes, crushed
- Chopped fresh cilantro, for serving

Directions

1. Set your cooking machine to cook at 183 degrees F.

2. Mix Brussels sprouts with olive oil, oyster sauce, brown sugar, sea salt flakes, ground black pepper, and red pepper flakes.

3. Add the mixture to a vacuum bag. Seal the bag using a vacuum sealer on the dry setting. Remove as much air as possible.

4. Place the bag in the water bath and set the timer for 35 minutes. You can serve it as a side dish or broil the Brussels sprouts until they are browned, 5 to 6 minutes.

5. Garnish with fresh chopped cilantro. Bon appétit

2. Asian-Style Vegetable Soup with Udon Noodles

8 Servings

Ready in about
2 hours 10 minutes

PER SERVING:
468 Calories; 4.4g Fat;
71.8g Carbs; 22.7g
Protein; 1.2g Sugars

Is there anything better than rich warm soup with fresh noodles? If you like a piquant flavor, drizzle each serving with the chili oil.

Ingredients

- 1 cup finely diced carrots
- 3/4 pound sweet potatoes, peeled and diced
- 2 tablespoons butter
- 5 ½ cups water
- 1 dried bay leaf
- 1 ¼ pounds Porcini mushrooms, thinly sliced
- 1/2 cup bamboo shoots from a can, drained and chopped

- 1 ½ cups shallots, minced
- 1 medium-sized garlic head, peeled and minced
- Salt and ground black pepper, to taste
- 1/2 teaspoon dried dill weed
- 1 tablespoon Japanese soy sauce
- 1 ½ tablespoons saké
- 1 ¼ pounds fresh Udon noodles
- 1 large handful spring onions, shredded

Directions

1. Firstly, preheat your device to 183 degrees F.

2. Take 1-quart vacuum bag and put in the carrots, sweet potatoes, and butter. Cook for 55 minutes. Reserve.

3. In another vacuum bag, combine the water, bay leaf, mushrooms, bamboo shoots, shallots and garlic. Seal the bag and place it in the water bath that is preheated to 185 degrees F; cook for 43 minutes; reserve.

4. Then, preheat your oven to 400 degrees F. Remove the sweet potatoes from the bag.

5. Arrange 1/2 of the sweet potatoes and carrots on a baking pan. Transfer the baking pan to the oven and bake for 9 minutes. Reserve.

6. In the meantime, puree the remaining sweet potatoes and carrots in a food processor.

7. Add the prepared mushroom mixture to a large-sized pot. Add the puréed mixture of sweet potatoes and carrots. Season with salt, pepper, and dill. Now, bring to a boil over high flame.

8. Add soy sauce, saké, and noodles. Serve in individual bowls garnished with spring onions and roasted sweet potatoes. Bon appétit!

3. FAMILY CREAMED CORN SOUP

6 Servings

Ready in about
2 hours 40 minutes

PER SERVING:
170 Calories; 10.3g Fat;
19.8g Carbs; 3.7g Protein;
3.4g Sugars

Serve this creamy soup as an impressive first course or whenever your family is craving a warm, hearty dish.

Ingredients

- 4 corn ears, husked
- 5 ½ cups water
- 1 ½ tablespoons extra-virgin olive oil
- 1 teaspoon sea salt flakes
- A few sprinkles of grated nutmeg
- 3/4 cup heavy cream
- 4 tablespoons minced chives, for serving

Directions

1. Set your cooker to 183 degrees F. Cut the kernels off the corn.

2. Add the corn cobs and water to the vacuum bag and seal it.

3. Then, place the corn kernels, olive oil, sea salt, and nutmeg into another bag. Seal the bag, removing as much air as possible and refrigerate until ready to use.

4. Cook the corn cobs for 2 hours; add the bag of corn kernel mixture in the last 25 minutes of the cooking time.

5. Add the liquid from the plastic bag of the corn kernels to a pot, reserving solids; pass through a chinois. Fold in heavy cream; simmer over a moderate heat, approximately 13 minutes.

6. Now, strain the liquid from the bag of corn cobs into the pot and stir to combine. Afterwards, add the corn kernels and serve warm garnished with fresh minced chives.

4. BUTTERY SPICED POACHED APPLES

4 Servings

Ready in about
1 hour 15 minutes

PER SERVING:
230 Calories; 12.1g Fat;
34.2g Carbs; 1.0g Protein;
24.6g Sugars

These apples are as appealing as they are delicious. Serve them in individual bowls, with dollops of crème fraîche, whipped cream or ice cream such as dulce de leche.

Ingredients

- 1 lemon
- 4 medium apples, peeled, cored, and diced
- 4 tablespoons butter, unsalted

- 1 teaspoon turmeric powder
- 1 teaspoon apple pie spice mix
- 1 teaspoon brown sugar

Directions

1. Cut the lemon and squeeze its juice over the apples.

2. Set your cooker to 180 degrees F.

3. Combine the apples with the remaining ingredients.

4. Place 1/2 of the apples in the vacuum bag; remove as much air as possible. Repeat with the remaining ingredients.

5. Place the bags in the sous vide chamber; cook for 1 hour 10 minutes. Serve warm.

5. Poached Pears in Honey and Moscato Wine Syrup

4 Servings

Ready in about
1 hour 20 minutes

PER SERVING:
536 Calories; 0.3g Fat;
96.9g Carbs; 1.0g Protein;
80.9g Sugars

Desserts cooked sous vide? How is it possible? Here are the best poached pears ever! Serve with gelato and enjoy!

Ingredients

- 4 Anjou pears
- 4 cups Moscato wine
- 1 (1-inch) piece fresh ginger, peeled, and finely chopped
- 1 ¾ cups of sugar

- 2 tablespoons of honey
- 2 cups of water
- 4-6 whole cloves
- 2 cinnamon sticks
- 1 teaspoon vanilla paste

Directions

1. Firstly, set your cooking machine to 180 degrees F. Peel your pears and set them aside.

2. Then, mix the wine, ginger, sugar, honey and water until everything is well incorporated. Divide the mixture among two large-sized vacuum seal bags.

3. Add two pears to each bag; divide the spices among the bags. Once the water bath has reached the desired temperature, add the prepared bags and allow to cook for 1 hour 10 minutes.

4. Now, transfer the pears to serving plates.

5. Strain the cooking liquid into a pan. Bring it to a simmer over a moderate flame; simmer for 8 to 10 minutes. Ladle over prepared pears. Bon appétit!

6. Skinny Spring Eggs

6 Servings

Ready in about
1 hour 20 minutes

PER SERVING:
146 Calories; 8.0g Fat;
11.3g Carbs; 9.5g Protein;
6.5g Sugars

If you're looking for a light veggie frittata, sous vide is here to help! Serve these fluffy eggs in jars and delight your family for Sunday brunch. Yummy!

Ingredients

- 1 ½ tablespoons of butter, room temperature
- 1 cup spring onions, finely chopped
- 2 spring garlic, minced
- 1 red bell pepper, deveined and chopped
- 1 green bell pepper, deveined and chopped
- 1 jalapeno pepper, deveined and chopped
- 1 large-sized carrot, trimmed and chopped
- 1 large-sized celery with leaves, trimmed and chopped

- 1 ½ cups cremini mushrooms, thinly sliced
- 2 heaping tablespoons fresh coriander, finely minced
- Salt and black pepper, to your liking
- 1/3 teaspoon smoked cayenne pepper
- A pinch of grated nutmeg
- 1/3 cup of milk
- 6 eggs

Directions

1. Set your machine to cook at 180 degrees F. Spritz 6 canning jars with a nonstick cooking spray.

2. Then, melt the butter in a cast-iron skillet that is preheated over medium-high flame. Sweat spring onions for about 4 minutes. Add the minced garlic and cook, stirring continuously, about 40 seconds or until just browned.

3. Next, stir in the peppers, carrot, and celery; cook until they have softened; it will take about 9 minutes.

4. Stir in the sliced mushrooms and sauté them for about 4 minutes. Add the coriander, salt, black pepper, cayenne pepper, and nutmeg; stir to combine well. Divide the sautéed mixture among your jars.

5. Now, beat the milk and eggs until frothy. Spoon the milk-egg mixture into the jars. Cover with the lids.

6. Once the water bath has reached the desired temperature, add the prepared jars and allow to cook for 1 hour. Allow them to slightly cool on a wire rack before serving. Taste and adjust the seasonings and serve with fresh, sliced radishes. Bon appétit!

7. Summer Pea Soup with Greek Yogurt

4 Servings

Ready in about
1 hour

PER SERVING:
130 Calories; 0.6g Fat;
26.2g Carbs; 6.5g Protein;
7.2g Sugars

When it's too hot to cook, we reach for chilled and refreshing soups. Greek yogurt provides a satisfying flavor that contrasts with the vegetables. Refreshingly easy!

Ingredients

- 1 cup shallots, chopped
- 2 cloves garlic, finely minced
- 1 carrot, trimmed and chopped
- 1 parsnip, trimmed and chopped
- 12 ounces of green peas, frozen
- 1 cup roasted vegetable stock
- 1 cup of water
- Salt and pepper, to taste
- 1 teaspoon dried or fresh dill weed
- 1/2 teaspoon fennel seeds
- 4 teaspoons of Greek-style yogurt, for garnish

Directions

1. Set your cooking machine to 183 degrees F.

2. Add the shallots, garlic, carrot, parsnip, and peas to a bag; cook for 55 minutes.

3. Now, puree the vegetables along with the stock, water, and seasonings in your food processor. Finally, transfer your soup to the refrigerator to chill.

4. Spoon into individual bowls. Top each serving with a swirl of Greek yogurt. Enjoy!

8. CREAMED WINTER SQUASH SOUP

4 Servings

Ready in about
1 hour 30 minutes

PER SERVING:
165 Calories; 3.7g Fat;
33.9g Carbs; 3.4g Protein;
2.2g Sugars

This recipe is super creamy and full of delicious flavors. It tastes even better the next day.

Ingredients

- 2 pounds of winter squash, peeled and diced
- 1 cup shallot, chopped
- 2 garlic cloves, peeled and pressed
- 1 teaspoon maple syrup
- 1/4 teaspoon freshly grated nutmeg
- Sea salt flakes and ground black pepper, to taste
- 1 cup of cream

Directions

1. Set your cooking machine to 183 degrees F.

2. Add the winter squash, shallot, and garlic to the cooking pouches and vacuum seal them. Let simmer for 1 hour 30 minutes.

3. Remove the vegetables from the cooking pouches. Puree them in your food processor, along with maple syrup, nutmeg, salt, pepper, and cream, until well combined.

4. Taste, adjust the seasonings and serve with Pepitas.

9. Broccoli and Cauliflower with Chili Cream Sauce

4 Servings

Ready in about
50 minutes

PER SERVING:
142 Calories; 11.1g Fat;
9.5g Carbs; 3.3g Protein;
2.9g Sugars

You can't go wrong with this simple vegetable side dish. You can serve these aromatic vegetables with fish tacos and turn the dish into the main course.

Ingredients

- 1/2 pound of broccoli, broken into florets
- 1/2 pound of cauliflower, broken into florets
- 1/2 teaspoon sea salt flakes
- 1/4 teaspoon ground black pepper, or more to taste
- 1/2 teaspoon cayenne pepper
- 2 tablespoons butter, melted
- 1 teaspoon dried tarragon
- 1/2 teaspoon bay leaf powder
- 1/4 teaspoon fennel seeds

For the Sauce:
- 2 tablespoons mayonnaise
- 4 tablespoons sour cream
- 1 tablespoon lemon juice
- 1 teaspoon chipotle chili sauce
- 1/2 teaspoon sea salt flakes

Directions

1. Set your cooker to 180 degrees F. Season broccoli and cauliflower with salt flakes, black pepper, and cayenne pepper.

2. Now, toss with melted butter, tarragon, bay leaf powder, and fennel seeds; toss to coat well. Add the vegetables to the cooking pouches; vacuum seal. Cook for 40 minutes.

3. Meanwhile, make the sauce by mixing all the sauce ingredients until well combined. Serve with warm broccoli and cauliflower. Bon appétit!

10. MUSHROOM AND MANCHEGO DELIGHT

4 Servings

Ready in about
1 hour 10 minutes

PER SERVING:
282 Calories; 23.5g Fat;
6.6g Carbs; 10.2g Protein;
2.4g Sugars

Good mushrooms deserve the best cheese! Manchego is a hard sheep's milk cheese with a buttery texture and nutty, tangy flavor. Give it a try!

Ingredients

- 4 tablespoons extra-virgin olive oil
- 1 pound cremini mushrooms
- 1 teaspoon kosher salt
- 1/4 teaspoon freshly ground black pepper
- 1/2 teaspoon dried dill weed

- 2 garlic cloves, pressed
- 2 spring onions, sliced
- 1/4 cup dessert wine
- 1 cup Manchego cheese, freshly grated

Directions

1. Set your cooker to 180 degrees F.

2. Add 2 tablespoons of olive oil, mushrooms, salt, pepper, and dill weed to a vacuum pouch. Now, seal the pouch and allow to sous vide for about 55 minutes.

3. Then, preheat a nonstick skillet over a moderate flame. Add the remaining 2 tablespoons of olive oil and swirl to coat the bottom.

4. Once hot, add the drained mushrooms, along with garlic and spring onions; sauté until tender and fragrant.

5. Add dessert wine to deglaze the pot and allow to simmer, uncovered, until all the liquid has evaporated. Serve topped with Manchego. Bon appétit!

11. Gourmet Root Vegetable Soup

8 Servings

Ready in about
2 hours 20 minutes

PER SERVING:
84 Calories; 0.9g Fat;
15.5g Carbs; 4.2g Protein;
4.5g Sugars

This is the perfect winter soup to warm you up immediately. Serve with herb croutons.

Ingredients

- 2 carrots, trimmed and diced
- 1 parsnip, trimmed and diced
- 1 stalk celery with leaves, diced
- 1 shallot, peeled and diced
- 2 garlic cloves, peeled

- 1 sprig rosemary
- 2 bay leaves
- Salt and ground black pepper, to your liking
- 5 cups vegetable stock
- 1 cup of water

Directions

1. Set your cooker to 183 degrees F. Place each type of vegetable into a separate vacuum pouch and seal.

2. Divide the remaining ingredients among the pouches; allow to sous vide for 2 hours 10 minutes. Strain liquid from the pouches into a large-sized pot, reserving the vegetables.

3. Let it simmer over a moderate flame for 8 to 12 minutes. Remove from the heat.

4. Add vegetables back to the pot and blend with an immersion blender; serve warm.

12. Buckwheat with Fennel and Cauliflower

6 Servings

Ready in about
35 minutes

PER SERVING:
210 Calories; 9.1g Fat;
28.8g Carbs; 3.6g Protein;
0.0g Sugars

Buckwheat is a nutrient-packed superfood that is available throughout the year and it is very easy to prepare. You can serve it as a good and healthy alternative to rice or quinoa.

Ingredients

- 1 large-sized fennel bulb, diced
- 4 tablespoons melted butter
- 1 lemon, freshly squeezed
- 1 cup cauliflower, cut into florets
- 2 tablespoons of balsamic vinegar
- 1 teaspoon sea salt flakes
- 1/2 teaspoon ground black pepper, or more to taste

- 1 teaspoon dried parsley flakes
- 1 teaspoon dried thyme
- 1/3 teaspoon dried marjoram
- 1 cup buckwheat, cooked
- 1 ½ tablespoons toasted walnuts, roughly chopped

Directions

1. Firstly, set your cooking machine to 183 degrees F.

2. Add the fennel, 2 tablespoons of butter and the lemon juice to a vacuum bag. Add the cauliflower, 2 remaining tablespoons of butter, and balsamic vinegar to another vacuum bag. Divide the seasonings among the bags.

3. Place the bags in the water bath; set the timer for 25 minutes. After that, remove the bags from the water bath.

4. Sear the fennel and cauliflower over a moderate heat until they are well browned. Add warm buckwheat and scatter toasted walnuts over everything. Bon appétit!

13. Vanilla and Cinnamon Poached Plums

3 Servings

Ready in about
30 minutes

PER SERVING:
317 Calories; 0.7g Fat;
83.7g Carbs; 1.7g Protein;
80.1g Sugars

Simple and aromatic poached plums are equally delicious served hot or chilled.
Serve with something creamy and enjoy!

Ingredients

- 9 ripe plums, halved and seeded
- 1/2 cup white sugar
- 1/2 cup brown sugar

- 1 cinnamon stick
- 1 vanilla pod, split and seeds scraped from middle

Directions

1. Set your cooking machine to 183 degrees F.

2. Place the plums in a single layer in a vacuum pouch. Add the remaining ingredients and seal.

3. Once the sous vide water bath has reached the desired temperature, insert the vacuum pouch of prepared plums; allow to cook for 20 minutes.

4. Serve immediately or place in the refrigerator until ready to serve. Bon appétit!

14. TANGY BRAISED CABBAGE

6 Servings

Ready in about
50 minutes

PER SERVING:
85 Calories; 3.7g Fat;
12.9g Carbs; 2.1g Protein;
5.9g Sugars

Inexpensive, healthy and delicious braised cabbage is one of the favorite sides all year round. However, you can serve it over fried eggs for a quick, complete meal.

Ingredients

- 1 head cabbage, outer leaves removed, cored, and shredded
- 1 red bell pepper, deveined and chopped
- 1 cup leeks, chopped
- 1 carrot, trimmed and chopped
- 2 garlic cloves, peeled and minced
- Sea salt, to taste
- 1 small-sized lemon, freshly squeezed
- 1 teaspoon berry jam
- 1 ½ tablespoons of extra-virgin olive oil
- 4-5 black peppercorns
- 1 bay leaf

Directions

1. Set your cooking machine to 185 degrees F.

2. Now, toss all ingredients in a large-sized mixing dish until everything is well coated.

3. Divide the mixture evenly among two vacuum bags and seal. Allow to sous vide for 50 minutes.

4. When the timer goes off, remove the bags from the water bath. Taste, adjust the seasonings and serve immediately.

15. Rainbow Veggie Bowl with Ginger Miso Dressing

6 Servings

Ready in about
2 hour 20 minutes

PER SERVING:
219 Calories; 17.5g Fat;
15.9g Carbs; 3.1g Protein;
3.4g Sugars

Cooked the traditional way, vegetables become dull in color. Vacuum packaging them for sous vide improves bright colors and great textures that can give a pop to your side dishes!

Ingredients

- 2 Roma tomatoes, diced
- 2 zucchinis, sliced
- 1 sweet pepper, deveined and thinly sliced
- 1 chili pepper, deveined and minced
- 2 small-sized shallots, peeled and diced
- 4 cloves garlic, peeled and crushed
- 4 tablespoons melted butter
- Salt and black pepper, to taste
- 1 teaspoon Hungarian paprika
- 1 teaspoon dried dill weed
- 1/2 teaspoon celery seeds

For Ginger Dressing:

- 2 tablespoons balsamic vinegar
- 1 tablespoon fresh ginger, peeled and grated
- 2 garlic cloves, peeled and minced
- A pinch of brown sugar
- 4 tablespoons olive oil

Directions

1. Set your cooker to 183 degrees F.

2. Put each type of vegetable into a separate vacuum seal bag. Divide the garlic, butter, and seasonings among the bags.

3. Seal the bags and transfer them to the water bath; cook for 40 minutes.

4. When the cooking time is up, remove the bag with the tomatoes. Adjust the timer for another 30 minutes.

5. When the cooking time is up, remove the bags with the zucchini and peppers. Set the timer for another 55 minutes to cook the shallots.

6. Chop all ingredients and toss them in a serving bowl.

7. Meanwhile, mix all ingredients for the ginger dressing. Drizzle over the prepared vegetables. Serve immediately.

CHICKEN

16. CHICKEN SOUP WITH SOBA NOODLES

6 Servings

Ready in about
2 hours 40 minutes

PER SERVING:
161 Calories; 5.4g Fat;
21.7g Carbs; 7.7g Protein;
4.1g Sugars

Flavorful pepper and root vegetables balance poultry meat in this tasty chicken soup! This is a true comfort food for the whole family.

Ingredients

- 1 yellow onion, peeled and sliced into rings
- 1 sweet pepper, deveined and sliced
- 1 parsnip, trimmed and chopped
- 1 carrot, trimmed and chopped
- 3 ½ cups kale
- 2 garlic cloves, minced
- 1 tablespoon soy sauce
- 1 (1-inch) piece ginger, peeled and thinly sliced
- 1 teaspoon shallot powder

- 1/2 teaspoon porcini powder
- Salt and ground black pepper, to your liking
- 1 teaspoon red pepper flakes, crushed
- 1/4 cup fresh coriander, coarsely chopped
- 1 ½ tablespoons of olive oil
- 1 chicken breast, boneless, skinless and cut into chunks
- 7 cups roasted vegetable stock
- 1 cup dried soba noodles

Directions

1. Set your cooker to 185 degrees F. In a mixing dish, mix all vegetables.

2. Then, add the soy sauce and ginger; season the vegetables with shallot powder, porcini powder, salt, black pepper, red pepper, and coriander; drizzle with olive oil.

3. Add the vegetable mixture to a large-sized zipper-lock bag; seal the bag; allow to sous vide for 1 hour 30 minutes. Allow it to cool completely.

4. Now, decrease the temperature of the water bath to 147 degrees F. Add the chicken to another bag and seal; allow to sous vide for 1 hour. Reserve.

5. Add roasted vegetable stock to a large-sized pot. Strain liquid from the cooking bags.

6. Bring the soup to a rapid boil; now, fold in soba noodles and cook until al dente.

7. Stir prepared vegetables and chicken into the pot; turn the heat to low. Let it simmer for about 6 minutes. Serve hot.

17. CHICKEN BREASTS IN BALSAMIC SAUCE

2 Servings

Ready in about
1 hour 20 minutes

PER SERVING:
215 Calories; 16.3g Fat;
2.6g Carbs; 13.8g Protein;
1.0g Sugars

Reserve the liquid stock for another use. For searing, use high-smoke-point oil like peanut oil or lard. Finish with a touch of balsamic vinegar to maximize the flavor.

Ingredients

- 1 medium-sized chicken breast, skinless and boneless
- 1 teaspoon sea salt flakes
- 1/4 teaspoon ground black pepper, or more to taste
- 1 tablespoon butter
- 1 teaspoon garlic powder

- 1 teaspoon onion powder
- 1/2 teaspoon mustard seeds
- 1 tablespoon peanut oil
- 2 tablespoons of balsamic vinegar
- 1/4 cup chicken broth
- 1 heaping tablespoon of fresh chopped parsley, for garnish

Directions

1. Set your cooker to 146 degrees F. Rinse the chicken and pat dry. Season with salt and black pepper; coat with butter on all sides.

2. Place the chicken breast in a cooking pouch; vacuum seal.

3. Cook for 1 hour; after that, remove the chicken from the cooking pouch and pat it dry. Sprinkle with garlic powder, onion powder, and mustard seeds.

4. Add peanut oil to a cast-iron skillet and swirl to coat the bottom; heat over a moderate heat. Once hot, add the chicken and allow it to sear for about 5 minutes. Flip the chicken once, and cook the other side for an additional 5 minutes or until it is golden browned.

18. Lemon-Dill Chicken Drumsticks

2 Servings

Ready in about
4 hours 10 minutes

PER SERVING:
367 Calories; 18.6g Fat;
3.5g Carbs; 45.4g Protein;
0.9g Sugars

If you love traditional roasted chicken drumsticks but have always wished they were juicy and stringy at the same time, sous vide chicken might be right for you!

Ingredients

- 2 skin-on chicken drumsticks, with bone
- 1□4 cup tamari sauce, divided
- 1 teaspoon garlic powder, divided
- 1 teaspoon kosher salt

- 1/4 teaspoon ground black pepper, or more to taste
- 1 teaspoon dill weed
- 2 tablespoons of olive oil
- Lemon wedges, to serve

Directions

1. Brush the chicken under the skin with tamari sauce. Rub garlic powder, salt, pepper, and dill weed into the chicken, under the skin.

2. Set your cooker to 173 degrees F. Add the chicken drumsticks to a cooking pouch and vacuum seal. Allow to sous vide for 4 hours.

3. Heat a heavy-bottomed skillet over a moderate flame; heat the oil. Place the chicken in the hot oil; cook until the chicken drumsticks are browned evenly on all sides, for 1 to 2 minutes.

4. Take the skillet off the heat and leave the flavors to infuse for 2 to 3 minutes before transferring to serving plates. Serve with fresh lemon wedges. Bon appétit!

19. HOT SPICY CHICKEN THIGHS

4 Servings

Ready in about
3 hours 10 minutes

PER SERVING:
251 Calories; 11.3g Fat;
2.1g Carbs; 33.2g Protein;
1.0g Sugars

These chicken thighs will change your perception of poultry. Tender, juicy, and flavorsome, they are sure to please.

Ingredients

- 1 tablespoon butter
- 1 pound chicken thighs
- Salt and ground black pepper, to taste
- 1 tablespoon tamari sauce
- 1 tablespoon balsamic vinegar

- 1 teaspoon molasses
- 2 cloves of garlic, finely minced
- 1 teaspoon hot pepper sauce
- 1/2 teaspoon dried marjoram

Directions

1. Set your cooker to 165 degrees F.

2. Toss all of the above ingredients in a large-sized mixing bowl; toss to coat well. Add all ingredients to a cooking pouch.

3. Seal the pouch and cook for 3 hours.

4. Line the bottom of the broiler pan with foil. Arrange the chicken wings on the broiler pan. Broil for 3 minutes; flip over and broil for another 3 minutes.

5. Serve with some extra hot sauce if desired. Bon appétit!

20. Thai-Style Chicken Legs with Sauce

3 Servings

Ready in about
1 hour 35 minutes

PER SERVING:
393 Calories; 22.5g Fat;
1.7g Carbs; 44.8g Protein;
1.2g Sugars

Looking for a chicken main dish recipe? You can have restaurant-style chicken legs at your own home! Bear in mind that nutritional information doesn't include Thai sweet chili sauce. Serve on toasted rolls!

Ingredients

- 3 skin-on chicken legs
- 3 tablespoons Asian fish sauce
- 1/2 tablespoon of fresh lemon juice
- 3 tablespoons olive oil
- 1 teaspoon mirin
- 1 teaspoon sea salt flakes
- 1/2 teaspoon freshly cracked mixed peppercorns
- 1/2 teaspoon cayenne pepper
- 1 tablespoon butter
- 2 tablespoons ground coriander
- Thai sweet chili sauce, to serve

Directions

1. Set your cooker to 150 degrees F. Place the chicken legs into a vacuum seal bag.

2. In a mixing dish, thoroughly combine the Asian fish sauce, lemon juice, olive oil, and mirin; whisk to combine well. Pour the sauce mixture over the chicken; seal the bag.

3. Allow to sous vide for 1 hour 30 minutes. When the timer goes off, remove the chicken from the bag, reserving the cooking liquid.

4. Season the chicken with salt, peppercorns, and cayenne pepper. Broil for about 5 minutes.

5. Heat a saucepan over a moderate heat; melt the butter. Once hot, add the cooking liquid; simmer until the sauce has thickened.

6. Serve over hot chicken legs, garnished with fresh coriander and Thai sweet chili sauce. Bon appétit!

21. Cheesy Chicken Meatballs in Tomato Sauce

8 Servings

Ready in about
1 hour

PER SERVING:
372 Calories; 22.0g Fat;
6.2g Carbs; 36.8g Protein;
3.8g Sugars

This kid-friendly recipe is the perfect game day appetizer. If you use
a canned tomato sauce, this becomes an easy-to-make meal. Serve with
toothpicks or skewers

Ingredients

- 1 ½ pounds ground chicken
- 6 ounces of cream cheese
- 1 cup fine breadcrumbs
- 1 egg white
- 1 ½ tablespoons fresh thyme leaves, finely chopped
- 1 small-sized onion, finely chopped
- 2 cloves of garlic, finely minced

- Salt and ground black pepper, to your liking
- 1/4 teaspoon celery seeds
- 1/2 teaspoon cayenne pepper
- 1 teaspoon Worcestershire sauce
- 1 ½ tablespoons of grapeseed oil
- 2 cups of tomato sauce, preferably homemade

Directions

1. Set your cooker to 146 degrees F.

2. In a mixing dish, thoroughly combine the ground chicken with cream cheese, breadcrumbs, egg white, thyme, onion, garlic, salt, black pepper, celery seeds, cayenne pepper, and Worcestershire sauce.

3. Shape the mixture into balls of similar size. Arrange the balls in a vacuum sealed bag in a single layer; seal according to manufacturer's instructions. Sous vide for 55 minutes. Now, pat each meatball dry.

4. Heat grapeseed oil in a nonstick skillet over medium-high heat until shimmering. Gently lay the meatballs in the skillet and cook until cooked on all sides, but still juicy and plump with a spring to the touch. Reserve.

5. Add tomato sauce to the same skillet and cook, stirring frequently, until warmed through or about 2 minutes. Serve with warm meatballs. Bon appétit!

22. GRANDMA'S WINTER CHICKEN STEW

6 Servings

Ready in about
3 hours

PER SERVING:
233 Calories; 7.2g Fat;
10.8g Carbs; 30.9g
Protein; 5.3g Sugars

Old-fashioned chicken stew is as delicious as it looks. Sous vide is one of the cooking methods that best retains nutrients.

Ingredients

- 1 ½ tablespoons of olive oil
- 3 garlic cloves, chopped
- 1 cup leeks, chopped
- 2 sweet peppers, deveined and chopped
- 1 Habanero pepper, deveined and chopped
- 1 celery stalk with leaves, trimmed and chopped
- 2 carrots, trimmed and diced
- 1 large-sized can of chopped tomatoes

- 2 tablespoons tomato puree
- 1 teaspoon kosher salt
- 1/2 teaspoon ground black pepper, or more to taste
- 1 teaspoon Hungarian paprika
- 2 bone-in chicken legs
- 2 bone-in chicken thighs
- 6 cups roasted vegetable stock

Directions

1. Preheat a nonstick skillet over a moderate flame; now, add the oil and swirl to coat the bottom of the skillet. Once hot, add the garlic and leeks; sauté until just tender and aromatic.

2. Add the remaining vegetables along with the tomato puree and seasonings. Turn the heat to low and simmer the mixture for 15 to 20 minutes or until it has thickened.

3. Transfer the sauce to a vacuum seal bag. Add the chicken. Set your cooker to 165 degrees F.

4. Allow to sous vide for 2 hours 30 minutes. Transfer the mixture from the bag to a large stock pot.

5. Add the vegetable stock and bring it to a rapid boil; reduce the heat and simmer over a medium-low heat for 15 minutes more. Ladle into individual bowls and serve hot.

23. SAGE GRILLED CHICKEN BREASTS

6 Servings

Ready in about
1 hour 35 minutes

PER SERVING:
347 Calories; 18.0g Fat;
0.0g Carbs; 43.7g Protein;
0.0g Sugars

Looking for a low-carb chicken recipe? Crispy, grilled chicken breast might be one of the most perfect family meals. Serve with your favorite salad.

Ingredients

- 3 tablespoons grapeseed oil
- 2 pounds of chicken breasts, boneless
- Salt and ground black pepper, to savor
- 1 teaspoon cumin powder

- 1 teaspoon dried marjoram
- 1 teaspoon red pepper flakes, crushed
- 2 heaping tablespoons sage leaves, roughly chopped

Directions

1. Set your cooker to 148 degrees F. Massage the oil into the flesh of the meat.

2. Season the chicken breasts with salt, pepper, cumin, marjoram, and red pepper flakes. Transfer the seasoned chicken into vacuum bags; divide sage leaves among the bags.

3. Allow to sous vide for 1 hour 30 minutes. Remove chicken breast from the bags and pat it dry using a kitchen towel.

4. Place the chicken on the hot side of the grill, and cook for 2 to 3 minutes. Flip them over and cook on the other side until skin is crisp and golden browned.

24. Gourmet Chicken Liver Spread

12 Servings

Ready in about
45 minutes +
chilling time

PER SERVING:
143 Calories; 7.3g Fat;
6.2g Carbs; 12.1g Protein;
2.5g Sugars

Just like grandma used to make a chicken spread! Slowly, healthy, with love...
Wrap what you don't eat and keep in the refrigerator.

Ingredients

- 1 ¼ pounds of chicken livers, trimmed of fat
- Sea salt flakes and freshly ground mixed peppercorns, to taste
- 1 teaspoon crushed red pepper flakes
- 1 teaspoon dried parsley flakes
- 1 teaspoon powdered sumac
- 1 teaspoon ground cumin
- 1 teaspoon ground coriander
- 1 teaspoon grapeseed oil

- 1 cup yellow onion, chopped
- 4 cloves of garlic, thinly sliced
- 1 cup tart apple, chopped
- 6 tablespoons of cognac
- 1 teaspoon pink peppercorns, freshly cracked
- Zest of 1 lemon
- 1 ½ teaspoons of fresh lemon juice
- 1 cup of heavy cream

Directions

1. Set your cooker to 155 degrees F.

2. Put the chicken livers in a very large vacuum bag; toss in the salt flakes, mixed peppercorns, red pepper, parsley flakes, sumac, cumin, and coriander.

3. Seal and place into the water bath. Allow to sous vide for 30 minutes.

4. Meanwhile, preheat a nonstick skillet over a moderate flame. Add the oil and swirl to coat the bottom of the skillet. Once hot, sweat the onion and garlic for about 4 minutes. Add the apples and cook until tender.

5. Pour in the cognac and stir to deglaze the pot; simmer over a medium-low flame until the mixture has thickened. Transfer the mixture into your food processor or blender.

6. Now, add the chicken livers to the blender. Add the pink peppercorns, lemon zest, and lemon juice. Puree until everything is completely blended and incorporated.

7. Then, whip the heavy cream and add it to the pureed apple/liver mixture. Keep in your refrigerator until ready to serve.

8. Drizzle with extra-virgin olive oil and serve with good crusty bread and cornichons. Bon appétit!

25. Risotto with Sticky Dijon Chicken Drumsticks

4 Servings

Ready in about
2 hours 20 minutes

PER SERVING:
361 Calories; 4.1g Fat;
49.9g Carbs; 27.1g
Protein; 1.1g Sugars

Chicken legs are affordable and tasty pieces of chicken! Moist and fluffy brown rice and succulent chicken legs work together to create a splendidly tasty family meal.

Ingredients

- 2 chicken legs, bone-in and skinless
- 1 teaspoon granulated garlic
- 1 teaspoon salt
- 1/2 teaspoon freshly ground black pepper
- 1 teaspoon coarse grain Dijon mustard
- 1 ¼ cups brown rice

- 1 cup of water
- 1 ½ cups vegetable stock
- 1 cup green onions, chopped
- A pinch of ground allspice
- 1/4 cup dry white wine
- 1 teaspoon agave syrup

Directions

1. Set your cooker to 165 degrees F. Pat chicken legs dry with a kitchen towel.

2. Put chicken legs into a bag, along with your granulated garlic, salt, black pepper, and Dijon mustard; seal. Allow to cook for 2 hours.

3. De-bone the chicken legs and reserve the meat.

4. Cook the rice with water and stock over a medium-high flame. Turn the heat to low, let it simmer, covered, until tender.

5. Now, preheat a cast-iron skillet over a moderate flame. Add the reserved chicken, green onions, and allspice; cook until heated through, about 4 minutes.

26. SPAGHETTI WITH CHICKEN MEATBALLS

4 Servings

Ready in about
2 hours

PER SERVING:
571 Calories; 16.1g
Fat; 64.2g Carbs; 40.1g
Protein; 0.9g Sugars

To prepare the perfect sous vide meatballs, don't sear them immediately after they are removed from the water bath. Let them cool to room temperature. And one more trick – make them the size of a chocolate truffle!

Ingredients

- 3/4 pounds of ground chicken
- 3/4 tablespoons of butter, melted
- 1 tablespoon Worcestershire sauce
- 3 garlic cloves, minced
- 2 tablespoons minced scallions
- 1/2 teaspoon dried basil
- 1/2 teaspoon dried tarragon
- 1/2 teaspoon fresh or dried ginger

- Sea salt and freshly cracked black pepper, to your liking
- 1/4 cup parmesan cheese, preferably freshly grated
- 1/4 cup unseasoned whole-wheat breadcrumbs
- 1 tablespoon of grapeseed oil
- 1 pack of spaghetti

Directions

1. Firstly, set your cooker to 148 degrees F.

2. Then, thoroughly mix the ground chicken with butter, Worcestershire sauce, garlic, scallion, basil, tarragon, ginger, salt, and black pepper.

3. Now, stir in the parmesan and breadcrumbs; mix again to combine well.

4. Shape the mixture into equal meatballs using oiled hands. Place the meatballs in a large vacuum bag; seal the bag.

5. Once the sous vide water bath has reached the desired temperature, insert the bag of meatballs and allow to cook for 1 hour 40 minutes.

6. Now, in a pan, heat the oil over a medium-high heat. Add the meatballs and fry them in batches until nicely browned all over; then, turn down the heat and fry until cooked through.

7. Meanwhile, cook the spaghetti according to the manufacturer's instructions and serve with the warm meatballs. Bon appétit!

27. Saucy Chicken with Cremini Mushrooms

4 Servings

Ready in about
3 hours

PER SERVING:
258 Calories; 11.1g Fat;
6.1g Carbs; 31.5g Protein;
1.9g Sugars

Cooking chicken breasts in the preheated water oven "locks" in the flavors and nutrients and makes it a great family meal. This is a delicious recipe you'll be asked to cook time and time again.

Ingredients

- 1 tablespoon of olive oil
- 2 chicken breasts, boneless and skinless
- Sea salt and ground black pepper, to taste
- 1 ½ tablespoons butter
- 1 cup scallion, finely chopped
- 3 garlic cloves, peeled and minced
- 10 ounces cremini mushrooms, sliced
- 1/2 teaspoon sea salt
- 1/4 teaspoon crushed red pepper flakes, or more to taste
- 1/2 teaspoon dried dill weed
- 1/2 teaspoon bay leaf powder
- 1/2 teaspoon cumin powder
- 3 tablespoons dry vermouth
- 1 tablespoon oyster sauce

Directions

1. Set your machine to 150 degrees F. Massage olive oil into the chicken meat. Season with salt and ground black pepper. Cut the chicken breasts into halves.

2. Add the chicken to a large-sized vacuum bag. Simmer for 1 to 3 hours; pat the chicken dry.

3. In a heavy-bottomed skillet, melt the butter over a moderate flame. Now, sauté the scallions and garlic until just tender and aromatic.

4. Throw in the mushrooms, salt, red pepper, dried dill weed, bay leaf powder, and cumin powder. Add the vermouth to deglaze the bottom of the skillet. Cook until the liquid has reduced by half.

5. Stir in oyster sauce, along with reserved chicken; let it simmer for a few more minutes or until heated through. Serve immediately and enjoy!

28. Chicken Sausage with Mashed Potatoes

4 Servings

Ready in about
2 hours 15 minutes
+ marinating time

PER SERVING:
330 Calories; 10.7g
Fat; 27.6g Carbs; 32.4g
Protein; 4.6g Sugars

Chicken sausage is flavored with spicy beer marinade. Potatoes cook right along the sausage, making it a complete meal.

Ingredients

- 2 links of smoked chicken sausage, casings removed

For the Marinade:

- 1/2 cup of beer
- 1 teaspoon sugar
- 1 tablespoon wine vinegar
- 1 tablespoon olive oil
- Salt and black pepper, to taste
- 1 teaspoon whole grain mustard
- 1/2 teaspoon Hungarian paprika
- 1 teaspoon dried marjoram
- 1 teaspoon cumin powder

- 1 teaspoon garlic powder
- 1 teaspoon onion powder

For the mashed Potatoes:

- 1 pound of baking potatoes, peeled and quartered
- 1/2 cup whole milk
- 1 tablespoon butter
- 1 teaspoon fine sea salt
- 1/4 teaspoon ground black pepper, or more to taste
- 1/2 teaspoon smoked cayenne pepper
- 1 heaping tablespoon fresh parsley, roughly chopped

Directions

1. In a large-sized mixing dish, combine all ingredients for the marinade. Now, add the sausage and marinate in your refrigerator for at least 3 hours.

2. Then, set your cooker to 150 degrees F. Allow it to sous vide for 2 hours 15 minutes. Reserve, keeping your sausage warm.

3. Meanwhile, add lightly salted water to a pot; bring to a rapid boil. Now, boil your potatoes until fork tender, after about 12 to 16 minutes; drain.

4. Now, warm the milk and butter in a pan that is preheated over low heat; blend the butter mixture into the cooked potatoes; blend with a potato masher until creamy and uniform.

5. Add the seasonings and serve immediately with prepared chicken sausage. Bon appétit!

29. FESTIVE CHICKEN SALAD

6 Servings

Ready in about
2 hours 20 minutes

PER SERVING:
308 Calories; 13.1g Fat;
5.9g Carbs; 40.0g Protein;
2.6g Sugars

With sous vide chicken that is done ahead of time, your festive dinner becomes a breeze! In this recipe, you can experiment with seasonings and vegetables and adjust them to suit your taste. Lovely!

Ingredients

- 4 medium-sized chicken breasts, cut into halves and fat trimmed
- 1 teaspoon salt
- 1/2 teaspoon freshly cracked black pepper
- 2 sprigs of rosemary, chopped
- 1 sprig of thyme, chopped
- 1 small-sized purple cabbage head, cored and thinly sliced
- 1 sweet pepper, deveined and thinly sliced

- 1 large-sized carrot, cut into matchsticks
- 1 tablespoon fresh cilantro, chopped
- 1 teaspoon minced garlic
- 1 tablespoon sesame oil
- 1 teaspoon chili powder
- 1 ½ tablespoons of oyster sauce
- 3 tablespoons of balsamic vinegar
- 1 cup fresh chives, chopped
- 1 tablespoon toasted sesame seeds

Directions

1. Set your cooker to 150 degrees F.

2. Divide chicken breast halves among 2 cooking pouches; add the salt, black pepper, rosemary, and thyme; vacuum seal your pouches.

3. Allow to sous vide for 2 hours. Remove the chicken pieces from the pouches; let them cool to room temperature.

4. Shred your chicken using two forks and transfer to a nice salad bowl; add the cabbage, pepper, carrots, cilantro, and minced garlic; toss to combine well.

5. In a small-sized mixing dish or a measuring cup, whisk sesame oil with chili powder, oyster sauce, and balsamic vinegar; whisk to combine well.

6. Next, drizzle the dressing over the salad and serve topped with fresh chives and toasted sesame seeds. Bon appétit!

30. Sweet and Sour Chicken Legs

4 Servings

Ready in about
4 hours

PER SERVING:
295 Calories; 7.1g Fat;
22.6g Carbs; 34.1g
Protein; 17.0g Sugars

This is the only recipe for sweet and sour sous vide chicken you'll ever need.
Because this combination of flavors will satisfy literally everyone.

- 1 orange
- 1/4 cup packed dark brown sugar
- 1/4 cup of red wine vinegar
- Salt and ground black pepper, to your liking
- 1/3 teaspoon Hungarian paprika

- 4 medium-sized chicken legs, bone-in
- 2 tablespoons all-purpose flour
- 4 garlic cloves, peeled and finely minced
- 1 tablespoon of olive oil
- 1/2 cup fresh flat-leaf parsley

Directions

1. Juice the orange into a bowl; add the sugar, vinegar, salt, pepper, and Hungarian paprika; whisk to combine well.

2. Mix the chicken with the flour; add to a zipper-lock bag. Now, stir in the sugar mixture and the garlic; shake to combine. Seal the bag according to manufacturer's instructions. Set your cooker to 165 degrees F.

3. When the water reaches the target temperature, lower the bag into the water bath; allow to sous vide for 4 hours.

4. Remove the chicken from the bag and carefully pat it dry with paper towels. Heat olive oil in a stainless-steel skillet over medium-high heat.

5. Cook until the chicken legs are golden brown and crisp, 1 to 2 minutes per side. Remove the bones with your fingertips, slice the chicken and serve immediately garnished with fresh parsley.

TURKEY & DUCK

31. Easy Juicy Turkey Drumsticks

4 Servings

Ready in about
20 minutes

PER SERVING:
225 Calories; 12.9g Fat;
27.3g Carbs; 2.8g Protein;
8.8g Sugars

Is there anything better than rich warm soup with fresh noodles? If you like a piquant flavor, drizzle each serving with the chili oil.

Ingredients

- Set your cooking machine to cook at 183 degrees F.

- Mix Brussels sprouts with olive oil, oyster sauce, brown sugar, sea salt flakes, ground black pepper, and red pepper flakes.

- Add the mixture to a vacuum bag. Seal the bag using a vacuum sealer on the dry setting. Remove as much air as possible.

- Place the bag in the water bath and set the timer for 35 minutes. You can serve it as a side dish or broil the Brussels sprouts until they are browned, 5 to 6 minutes.

- Garnish with fresh chopped cilantro. Bon appétit!

Directions

1. Set your cooking machine to cook at 183 degrees F.

2. Mix Brussels sprouts with olive oil, oyster sauce, brown sugar, sea salt flakes, ground black pepper, and red pepper flakes.

3. Add the mixture to a vacuum bag. Seal the bag using a vacuum sealer on the dry setting. Remove as much air as possible.

4. Place the bag in the water bath and set the timer for 35 minutes. You can serve it as a side dish or broil the Brussels sprouts until they are browned, 5 to 6 minutes.

5. Garnish with fresh chopped cilantro. Bon appétit!

32. GRILLED CAJUN TURKEY THIGHS

4 Servings

Ready in about
10 hours

PER SERVING:
301 Calories; 12.6g Fat;
0.2g Carbs; 44.0g Protein;
0.0g Sugars

Looking for Thanksgiving main course recipes? Here're wonderfully juicy, perfectly grilled turkey thighs. Serve with pea purée and enough salad.

Ingredients

- 4 turkey thighs
- 1 tablespoon Cajun seasoning
- 1 teaspoon sea salt flakes
- 1/2 teaspoon freshly ground black pepper

- 2 sprigs of fresh rosemary
- 4-5 mixed peppercorns
- 2 bay leaves
- 1 ½ tablespoons of grapeseed oil

Directions

1. Set your cooker to 165 degrees F.

2. Sprinkle the turkey thighs with Cajun seasoning, salt, and black pepper. Place in a vacuum seal bag; add the rosemary, mixed peppercorns, and bay leaves. Seal the bag.

3. Allow it to sous vide for 10 hours; keep the turkey thighs submerged. Once cooking is complete, remove the turkey thighs from the bag and pat them dry.

4. Prepare grill for direct-heat cooking over medium-hot charcoal. Grease a grill rack; grease the turkey thighs with grapeseed oil. Grill them until crisp, turning twice; serve immediately.

33. Amazingly Succulent Turkey Lettuce Wraps

4 Servings

Ready in about
2 hours

PER SERVING:
287 Calories; 14.4g
Fat; 16.8g Carbs; 30.9g
Protein; 3.1g Sugars

Here's a refreshing and delicious recipe for lettuce wraps. You can substitute bibb lettuce for butter lettuce. They both have sturdy leaves that are just perfect for these wraps.

Ingredients

- 1 turkey breast, boneless and skinless
- 4 garlic cloves, minced
- 1 teaspoon sea salt
- Freshly cracked black pepper, to taste
- 1 large-sized bibb lettuce head
- 2 tablespoons of Worcestershire sauce

- 2 tablespoons of wine vinegar
- 1 ½ teaspoons of sriracha
- 2 tablespoons of olive oil
- 2 tablespoons toasted sesame seeds
- 4 scallions, chopped

Directions

1. Set your cooker to 150 degrees F. Pat turkey breast dry.

2. Mash garlic to a paste with salt in a mortar and pestle. Spread it evenly over the turkey breast. Add the turkey breast to a vacuum seal bag, along with black pepper; seal it according to manufacturer's instructions.

3. Place the bag in the water bath and set the timer for 1 hour 30 minutes. Remove the turkey from the bag, and shred the meat using a stand mixer. Reserve in a bowl.

4. Then, core, wash, and separate the bibb lettuce.

5. In a mixing dish, whisk Worcestershire sauce, wine vinegar, sriracha, olive oil, and toasted sesame seeds; reserve.

6. Preheat a nonstick skillet over a medium-high flame; briefly sauté the scallions until just tender and fragrant. Add the shredded turkey and stir until heated through.

7. Scoop up a big spoonful of turkey mixture and place it in the middle of a lettuce leaf. Repeat with the remaining ingredients.

8. Drizzle with sauce and transfer to a serving platter. Bon appétit!

34. TURKEY MEATBALLS WITH COOL MINT YOGURT SAUCE

4 Servings

Ready in about
1 hour 10 minutes

PER SERVING:
213 Calories; 8.3g Fat;
10.4g Carbs; 22.8g
Protein; 5.0g Sugars

These meatballs use only the most basic pantry staples and take 5 minutes to prepare. They are juicy, soft and wonderful. Make this recipe a true Greek feast by spreading the mint-yogurt sauce on pieces of pita.

Ingredients

- 3/4 pound of lean ground turkey
- 2 garlic cloves, finely minced
- 2 scallions, finely chopped
- 1 teaspoon sea salt
- 1/4 teaspoon black pepper, or more to taste
- 1/2 teaspoon cayenne pepper

- 1 teaspoon dried parsley flakes
- 1/4 cup fresh white breadcrumbs
- 1 medium-sized egg, beaten
- 1 cup Greek yogurt
- 8 fresh mint leaves, finely minced

Directions

1. Set your cooker to 147 degrees F.

2. In a mixing dish, thoroughly combine the ground turkey with garlic, scallions, salt, black pepper, cayenne pepper, parsley flakes, and breadcrumbs; knead well.

3. Now, add the egg and mix until everything is well combined. Shape the mixture into 28 to 30 meatballs (about 1-inch in diameter). Place the meatballs in a single layer in vacuum sealed bags.

4. Once the sous vide water bath has reached the target temperature, add the bag of meatballs; allow them to sous vide for 1 hour. Remove turkey meatballs from the bags.

5. Lightly grease a sheet pan with a nonstick cooking oil. Arrange the meatballs on the pan; bake in batches as required. Bake for about 7 minutes or until golden brown.

6. In the meantime, make the sauce by mixing Greek yogurt with mint leaves. Serve mint yogurt sauce alongside the baked meatballs. Enjoy!

35. Mediterranean-Style Turkey Legs

6 Servings

Ready in about
8 hours

PER SERVING:
416 Calories; 13.6g Fat;
71.5g Carbs; 9.3g Protein;
3.4g Sugars

Marinating overnight and cooking this turkey meat slowly keeps it moist and flavorful. Extremely juicy and tender with a dash of high-quality herbs, these are not entry-level turkey legs. Serve with Aioli and enjoy!

Ingredients

- 2 bone-in turkey legs, skinless
- 1 teaspoon fresh or dried ginger, peeled and minced
- 1 tablespoon fresh coriander, minced
- 1 teaspoon dried oregano
- 1/4 teaspoon cumin powder
- 1/2 teaspoon ground cinnamon
- Sea salt and ground black pepper, to your liking

- 2 sprigs of rosemary, chopped
- 2 garlic cloves, minced
- 2 tablespoons of whole-grain mustard
- 2 tablespoons of olive oil
- 2 medium-sized fresh lemons, juiced
- 1 ½ tablespoons of butter

Directions

1. Toss the turkey legs with the minced ginger, coriander, oregano, cumin powder, cinnamon, salt, black pepper, and rosemary.

2. In a separate dish, combine the garlic, mustard, olive oil, and lemon juice; whisk to combine well. Add this garlic mixture to the herb mixture. Whisk again until everything is well combined. Add the turkey legs and marinate overnight.

3. Place the turkey legs in vacuum seal bags; seal the bags.

4. Now, set your cooker to 165 degrees F. Lower the bag into the hot water and allow to sous vide for 8 hours.

5. Remove the bags from the water bath; pat turkey legs dry. Melt the butter in a sauté pan that is preheated over a moderate heat. Cook turkey legs for 2 to 3 minutes on each side or until heated through. Bon appétit!

37. ANGEL HAIR TURKEY SOUP

8 Servings

Ready in about
8 hours 30 minutes

PER SERVING:
291 Calories; 5.1g Fat;
31.2g Carbs; 28.4g
Protein; 2.1g Sugars

There is no better way to warm up in the winter than with a bowl of hot soup. This is a rich and comforting turkey soup full of fresh vegetables and tender turkey meat.

Ingredients

- 3 bone-in turkey thighs
- 1 teaspoon kosher salt
- 1/2 teaspoon ground black pepper
- 1 teaspoon marjoram, fresh or dried
- 1 cup shallots, chopped
- 1 celery stalk with leaves, trimmed and chopped
- 2 carrots, trimmed chopped

- 6 cups of vegetable stock
- 2 bay leaves
- 1 teaspoon dried parsley flakes
- 1/2 teaspoon garlic powder
- 2 bouillon cubes
- 2 cups angel hair, cooked

Directions

1. Set your cooker to 165 degrees F.

2. Season the turkey thighs with salt, black pepper, and marjoram. Add the seasoned turkey in a zip lock bag and seal it.

3. Next, lower the bag into the water bath; cook the turkey for 8 hours. Debone the turkey thighs and pull the meat apart with two forks; reserve.

4. In a large-sized stockpot that is preheated over a moderate flame, sauté the shallots until just tender and aromatic. Now, add the celery and carrot and continue sautéing until they have softened.

5. Add a splash of vegetable stock to deglaze the bottom of your pot. Now, stir in the bay leaves, parsley flakes, garlic powder, and bouillon cubes; add the remaining stock and bring to a rapid boil.

6. Decrease the heat to simmer; simmer for 15 minutes longer or until everything is warmed through. Add the cooked angel hair pasta and reserved turkey meat to the hot soup. Serve immediately!

38. Holiday Herby Turkey Roulade

6 Servings

Ready in about
5 hours 15 minutes

PER SERVING:
444 Calories; 12.0g
Fat; 15.9g Carbs; 64.6g
Protein; 1.3g Sugars

This recipe is the holy grail for anyone in search of a sophisticated Thanksgiving turkey recipe. Feel free to experiment with seasonings and serve the best-roasted and the moistest turkey ever!

Ingredients

- 1 whole turkey breast, boned and butterflied
- 3 tablespoons butter, melted
- 1 teaspoon kosher salt
- 1/2 teaspoon ground black pepper
- 1 teaspoon dried rosemary
- 1/2 teaspoon bay leaf powder
- 1 teaspoon mustard seeds

Directions

1. Set your cooker to 150 degrees F. Then, rub the turkey breast with melted butter.

2. Season the turkey breast with the salt, pepper, rosemary, bay leaf powder, and mustard seeds. Then, roll up the turkey breast tightly using a plastic wrap and toothpicks. Use cooking twine to tie the ends of the roulade.

3. Place your roulade in a vacuum seal bag; seal the bag and lower it into the water bath; allow to sous vide for 5 hours.

4. Remove the bag from the water and unwrap the meat. Lastly, roast it in the preheated oven at 475 degrees F for 9 to 12 minutes.

5. Allow it to rest at room temperature before slicing. Serve warm with side dishes of choice. Bon appétit!

39. MOM'S CREAMED TURKEY SALAD

8 Servings

Ready in about
3 hours 35 minutes

PER SERVING:
465 Calories; 16.8g Fat;
7.4g Carbs; 67.7g Protein;
2.8g Sugars

Sous vide is a fantastic method for cooking holiday meat recipes. The roasts are tender, juicy and flavorful. It also frees up your oven and stove for other recipes. Win-win!

Ingredients

- 1 medium-sized turkey breast, skinless
- 1 teaspoon fine sea salt
- 1/4 teaspoon cracked mixed peppercorns, or more to taste
- 1/2 teaspoon red pepper flakes
- 4 scallions, chopped

- 1/2 head of shredded cabbage
- 1/2 cup of mayonnaise
- 1/4 cup of Dijon mustard
- 2 tablespoons of balsamic vinegar
- 1 tablespoon fresh orange juice
- Toasted pine nuts, to serve

Directions

1. Debone the turkey breast and cut into halves. Then, season with salt, mixed peppercorns, and red pepper flakes.

2. Add to a vacuum bag and seal according to manufacturer's instructions.

3. Next step, set your cooker to 150 degrees F. Now, lower the sealed bag into the water bath. Let your turkey cook for 3 hours.

4. Lastly, bake in the preheated oven at 395 degrees F approximately 35 minutes. Allow the turkey to cool slightly before slicing. After that, cut the turkey into strips and transfer to a large-sized salad bowl.

5. Stir in scallions and shredded cabbage; stir to combine. Add the mayonnaise, mustard, vinegar, and orange juice. Gently and slowly stir until everything is well incorporated.

6. Afterward, garnish with pine nuts and serve with enough corn bread or garlic croutons.

40. Exotic Za'atar Pita Burgers

6 Servings

Ready in about
1 hour 20 minutes

PER SERVING:
355 Calories; 11.2g
Fat; 35.2g Carbs; 28.2g
Protein; 1.2g Sugars

Za'atar is a Middle Eastern spice mix composed of sumac and sesame, along with a bit of salt and dried herbs. Serve these exotic, juicy burgers with zucchini fries and dollops of tzatziki. Enjoy!

Ingredients

- 1 ½ pounds of lean ground turkey
- 1 tablespoon olive oil
- 2 garlic cloves, minced
- 1 cup green onions, chopped
- 1 tablespoon Za'atar
- 2 tablespoons of fresh coriander, minced
- 1 ½ tablespoons of oyster sauce

- 1 (1-inch) piece of fresh ginger, peeled and grated
- 1 teaspoon kosher salt
- 1/2 teaspoon ground black pepper
- 6 pita breads
- Pickles, to serve

Directions

1. In a mixing dish, thoroughly combine the ground turkey with olive oil, garlic, green onions, Za'atar, coriander, oyster sauce, ginger, salt and black pepper.

2. Shape into 6 equal patties. Cover and place in your freezer for 4 hours. After that, set your cooker to 146 degrees F.

3. Place each patty in a separate vacuum seal bag and seal it. Allow to sous vide for 1 hour 15 minutes.

4. Add the patties to the pan and cook to desired doneness. Meanwhile, slice each pita in half and toast them for approximately 2 minutes. Arrange warm pitas with burgers and pickles. Bon appétit!

41. Sophisticated Duck Breasts with Raspberry Sauce

6 Servings

Ready in about
1 hour 45 minutes

PER SERVING:
343 Calories; 20.4g Fat;
2.8g Carbs; 31.8g Protein;
0.8g Sugars

Delicious and juicy duck breasts topped with tangy raspberry-wine sauce. Serve as a main course for any occasion and your family and guests will enjoy this moist and flavorful poultry recipe.

Ingredients

- 1 ½ tablespoons of peanut oil
- 3/4 cup of green onions, finely chopped
- 2 teaspoons of minced garlic
- 1/2 cup ruby port
- 1 tablespoon raspberry vinegar
- 3/4 tablespoon Dijon mustard
- 1/3 cup raspberries

- 3 duck breasts, boneless
- 1 teaspoon salt
- 1/2 teaspoon smoked cayenne pepper
- 1/2 teaspoon freshly cracked mixed peppercorns
- 1/2 teaspoon dried rosemary
- 1 teaspoon dried tarragon
- 1 tablespoon melted butter

Directions

1. Using a sharp knife, make a crisscross pattern on the duck skin.

2. Then, warm the peanut oil in a pot that is preheated over a moderate heat. Once hot, sauté the green onions and garlic for about 4 minutes or until they are just tender.

3. After that, add ruby port and raspberry vinegar; stir to scrape up brown bits from the bottom of your pot. Throw in raspberries, stirring constantly to break them up. Reserve.

4. Sprinkle the duck breasts on all sides with salt, cayenne pepper, cracked peppercorns, rosemary, and tarragon. Then, place the seasoned duck breasts in vacuum bags.

5. Set your cooking machine to 140 degrees F; allow to sous vide for 1 hour 30 minutes. Remove the duck from bags and pat them dry.

6. Next, melt the butter in a nonstick skillet over a moderate heat. Then, cook the duck breasts, skin side down, about 5 minutes or until the skin is crisp.

7. Flip the duck breasts over and cook on the other side for a further 3 minutes. Allow them to rest for 5 to 10 minutes before slicing.

8. Cut the duck breasts into slices, spoon raspberry sauce over them and serve right away. Bon appétit!

42. Herbed Roast Duck Drumsticks

4 Servings

Ready in about
8 hour 40 minutes

PER SERVING:
393 Calories; 27.1g Fat;
0.3g Carbs; 35.3g Protein;
0.0g Sugars

Is there anything better than rich warm soup with fresh noodles? If you like a piquant flavor, drizzle each serving with the chili oil.

Ingredients

- 3 tablespoons of grapeseed oil
- 3 duck drumsticks
- 1 teaspoon dried rosemary
- Salt and black pepper, to taste
- 1/2 teaspoon cayenne pepper

Directions

1. Warm 2 tablespoons of grapeseed oil in a heavy-bottomed skillet that is preheated over a moderate flame. Now, sear duck drumsticks for 2 to 3 minutes on each side.

2. Then, add the duck drumsticks to vacuum bags; add 1 remaining tablespoon of oil, rosemary, salt, black pepper, and cayenne pepper; seal the bags.

3. Meanwhile, set your device to 165 degrees F. Now, slowly lower the bags into a container of water. Allow to sous vide for 8 hours.

4. Afterward, arrange the duck drumsticks on a lightly greased baking pan. Roast for about 40 minutes, flipping once or twice. Serve right away.

43. MELT-IN-YOUR-MOUTH DUCK BREAST

4 Servings

Ready in about
1 hours 40 minutes
+ marinating time

PER SERVING:
347 Calories; 14.7g
Fat; 30.7g Carbs; 23.9g
Protein; 29.5g Sugars

Is there anything better than rich warm soup with fresh noodles? If you like a piquant flavor, drizzle each serving with the chili oil.

Ingredients

- 6 cups of water
- 1/2 cup sugar
- 1 tablespoon honey
- 2 tablespoons of sea salt flakes
- 1 teaspoon ground black pepper
- 1 tablespoon whole-grain mustard
- 1/2 teaspoon bay leaf powder

- 1 teaspoon cumin powder
- 1 teaspoon celery seeds
- 1 teaspoon garlic powder
- 1 teaspoon shallot powder
- 2 small-sized duck breasts, cut into halves
- 1 tablespoon lard

Directions

1. Bring 2 cups of water to a rapid boil. In a mixing dish, thoroughly combine sugar, honey, sea salt flakes, black pepper, mustard, bay leaf powder, cumin powder, celery seeds, garlic powder, and shallot powder.

2. Pour in the remaining water. Add the duck breasts to the marinade. Place in the refrigerator for about 4 hours. Pat them dry and place in a vacuum bag.

3. Set your device to 145 degrees F. Seal the bag and cook for 90 minutes. Let it rest for about 10 minutes.

4. Cut into slices. Melt the lard in a pan; once hot, sear the duck breasts until crisp and browned. Bon appétit!

44. Duck and Vegetable Soup with Soba Noodles

6 Servings

Ready in about
2 hours

PER SERVING:
303 Calories; 10.6g
Fat; 31.4g Carbs; 22.1g
Protein; 0.6g Sugars

Perfect for festive dinner, this recipe is certain to wow your family and guests.
You can experiment with seasonings.

Ingredients

- 2 duck breasts, filleted

For the Marinade:

- 1 ½ tablespoons of rice vinegar
- 2 garlic cloves, finely minced
- 1 tablespoon tamari sauce
- 1 teaspoon kosher salt
- 1/2 teaspoon ground black pepper, or more to taste
- A pinch of ground allspice

For the Soup:

- 1 tablespoon olive oil
- 1/2 cup shallots, chopped
- 1 large-sized carrot, trimmed and chopped
- 1 celery stalk with leaves, trimmed and chopped
- 5 cups of vegetable stock
- 1/2 pound Soba noodles, cooked

Directions

1. Pat duck fillets dry with kitchen towel. Whisk all ingredients for the marinade in a mixing bowl.

2. Next, add the duck meat to the bowl and let it marinate overnight in your refrigerator.

3. The next day, set the cooker to 140 degrees F. Place marinated duck fillets in a vacuum bag. Allow to sous vide for 1 hour 30 minutes; let it cool slightly before slicing. Now, shred the meat with two forks and reserve.

4. In a large-sized stock pot, heat olive oil over a moderate flame; now, sauté the shallots, carrot, and celery until just tender. Pour in vegetable stock and bring to a boil.

5. Reduce to a simmer; let it simmer until heated through. Add cooked noodles and reserved duck meat to the hot soup and serve right away. Bon appétit!

45. Tacos de Carnitas de Pato

8 Servings

Ready in about
8 hours

PER SERVING:
338 Calories; 18.6g
Fat; 17.1g Carbs; 26.2g
Protein; 2.4g Sugars

Here's an all-star taco recipe with slowly braised duck legs, homemade salsa, and warm corn tortillas. Perfect for your taco night!

Ingredients

For the Duck Legs:

- 4 bone-in duck legs
- 2 tablespoons of sea salt flakes
- 1 teaspoon red pepper flakes, crushed
- 1 teaspoon black pepper
- 1 teaspoon Five-spice powder
- 1 tablespoon lard
- 1/2 cup tamarind sauce

For the Salsa:

- 2 tomatillos, chopped
- 2 tomatoes, chopped
- 4 green onions, minced
- 2 garlic cloves, minced
- 1 sweet pepper, deveined and chopped
- 1 habanero pepper, deveined and chopped
- 1/2 cup of chopped fresh cilantro
- 1 tablespoon fresh lemon juice

For the Tacos:

- 8 corn tortillas
- 1 avocado, peeled and sliced

Directions

1. Sprinkle the duck legs with salt, red pepper and black pepper on all sides. Let them stand in your refrigerator overnight.

2. Add duck legs to vacuum bags; seal. Set the cooker to 165 degrees F. Allow to sous vide for 8 hours. Remove the bags from the water bath and let the meat slightly cool. Shred the duck meat into chunks, discarding skin and bone.

3. Season duck legs with Five-spice powder. Melt the lard in a cast-iron skillet. Sear duck legs until slightly crispy. Add tamarind sauce and continue cooking until warmed through. Pile into warm tortillas.

4. Meanwhile, make the salsa by preheating a saucepan. Now, cook the tomatillos, tomatoes, green onions, and garlic over a medium flame.

5. Allow to cool slightly and transfer to a food processor; add the peppers, cilantro, and lemon juice. Purée until well blended and uniform.

6. Top each taco with avocado slices and serve with salsa on the side.

PORK

46. Juicy Pork Cutlets with Sautéed Vegetables

8 Servings

Ready in about
4 hours

PER SERVING:
239 Calories; 7.5g Fat;
3.4g Carbs; 37.6g Protein;
1.7g Sugars

Pork cutlets cooked sous vide results in meat with a great texture. They go well with a side dish such as mashed potatoes.

Ingredients

- 2 ½ pounds of pork cutlets
- 1 teaspoon fine sea salt
- 1/2 teaspoon freshly cracked black pepper
- 2 sprigs of thyme, chopped
- 2 sprigs of rosemary, chopped
- 1/2 teaspoon cayenne pepper

- 1 ½ tablespoons of lard
- 4 scallions, chopped
- 4 garlic cloves, peeled and minced
- 1 red bell pepper, deveined and thinly sliced
- 1 green bell pepper, deveined and thinly sliced

Directions

1. Salt and pepper the pork cutlets; sprinkle with thyme, rosemary and cayenne pepper. Add to sous vide pouches and seal them.

2. Cook at 150 degrees F for 4 hours. Remove pork from the pouches; pat them dry with a dish cloth.

3. Melt the lard in a stainless-steel skillet over a moderate heat. Quickly sear the cutlets for about 2 minutes per side, until nicely browned.

4. Now, in the remaining liquid in the pan, sauté the scallions until just tender. Throw in the garlic and peppers; continue sautéing until tender and aromatic.

5. Taste, adjust the seasonings, and serve over pork cutlets. Bon appétit!

47. The Best Pork Loin Roast Ever

6 Servings

Ready in about
3 hours

PER SERVING:
384 Calories; 24.1g Fat;
0.5 Carbs; 38.9g Protein;
0.0g Sugars

Cooking with sous vide allows you to keep the entire roast the doneness you want. If you want medium-rare, use between 130 and 135 degrees F; for medium – use 140 to 150 degrees F. If you like dry meat with a tacky texture, preheat the machine to 160 degrees F. Lovely!

Ingredients

- 1 ¼ pounds of pork loin
- 1 teaspoon fine sea salt
- 1/2 teaspoon mixed peppercorns, freshly cracked
- 1 teaspoon dried parsley flakes
- 1/2 teaspoon onion powder

- 1 teaspoon fresh oregano, minced
- 1 tablespoon fresh basil, minced
- 1 tablespoon fresh coriander, minced
- 2 green garlic, minced
- 1 ½ tablespoons of butter, softened

Directions

1. Set your cooking machine to 160 degrees F.

2. Sprinkle the pork loin with salt, cracked peppercorns, parsley, and onion powder. Add them to sous vide bags; add herbs and green garlic, and shake to distribute evenly. Seal bags.

3. Allow to sous vide for 3 hours.

4. Meanwhile, preheat your oven to 350 degrees F. Butter the meat on all sides. Place in the baking pan, and roast, basting with pan liquids. Roast until it is browned. Check for doneness; remember – any juices that run out should be clear.

5. Transfer the pork loin to a cutting board and tent with foil for 10 minutes. Cut into thick slices and serve immediately. Bon appétit!

48. Garlicky Herby Spare Ribs

4 Servings

Ready in about
12 hours

PER SERVING:
274 Calories; 9.5g Fat;
14.9g Carbs; 30.9g
Protein; 4.9g Sugars

Is there anything better than rich warm soup with fresh noodles? If you like a piquant flavor, drizzle each serving with the chili oil.

Ingredients

- 1 pound of spare ribs
- 1 teaspoon fine sea salt
- 1/2 teaspoon mixed peppercorns, freshly cracked
- 1 ½ tablespoons of olive oil
- 1 shallot, peeled and chopped
- 1 carrot, cleaned and chopped
- 1 celery stalk with leaves, chopped
- 1 parsnip, cleaned and chopped
- 1 ½ tablespoons of rice wine vinegar
- 1 teaspoon dried rosemary
- 1 teaspoon dried marjoram
- 1 teaspoon dried basil
- 3 garlic cloves, minced

Directions

1. Set your cooker to 160 degrees F.

2. Now, sprinkle the spare ribs with salt and cracked peppercorns. Place the ribs in vacuum seal bags. Seal the bags; allow to sous vide for 12 hours.

3. In the meantime, heat 1 tablespoon of olive oil in a saucepan that is preheated over a moderate heat. Once hot, sauté the shallot until tender and fragrant. Now, add the carrot, celery, and parsnip. Continue sautéing until they have softened.

4. Add the rice wine vinegar and stir to deglaze the bottom of the pan. Now, remove the bags from the water bath. Remove the spare ribs from the bag; pat dry with a dish cloth.

5. Warm remaining 1/2 tablespoon of olive oil. Sear the pork along with the remaining herbs and garlic. Serve over sautéed vegetables. Bon appétit!

49. TENDER PORK LOIN ROAST WITH GARLIC

4 Servings

Ready in about
4 hours

PER SERVING:
257 Calories; 10.8g Fat;
0.6g Carbs; 37.3g Protein;
0.0g Sugars

Here're buttery, tender pork fillets for any occasion! They go perfectly with horseradish or mustard. Use leftovers for sandwiches.

Ingredients

- 1 ¼ pounds of pork fillet
- 1 small-sized garlic clove, peeled and thinly sliced
- 1/2 teaspoon sea salt flakes
- 1/2 teaspoon cayenne pepper
- 1/4 teaspoon ground black pepper

- 1 teaspoon dried oregano
- 1 teaspoon dried basil
- 1 teaspoon dried thyme
- 2 tablespoons of butter
- Fresh, chopped chives, to serve

Directions

1. Firstly, set your cooker to 160 degrees F. Use a sharp paring knife to make a dozen small slits in the pork meat. Tuck garlic slivers into slits.

2. Then, sprinkle pork loin with salt, cayenne pepper, and black pepper. Add to zipper-lock bags; throw in the oregano, basil, and thyme.

3. Place the bags in the water bath. Allow to sous vide for 3 to 4 hours. Pat it dry with a dish cloth and grease with butter on all sides.

4. Place the pork fillets in the preheated oven. Roast at 350 degrees F until the crust is done, about 5 minutes. Transfer to a serving platter.

5. Scatter chopped chives over the pork fillet and serve warm. Bon appétit!

50. HOLIDAY SEARED PORK BUTT

8 Servings

Ready in about
24 hours

PER SERVING:
227 Calories; 7.6g Fat;
6.4g Carbs; 30.3g Protein;
5.1g Sugars

Everyone loves seared pork! However, searing requires high temperature so the outside of your meat will burn before the inside finishes cooking. Therefore, we use the amazing sous vide technique in this recipe. Enjoy!

Ingredients

- 2 pounds of pork Boston butt, cut into pieces
- Sea salt and ground black pepper, to your liking
- 2 tablespoons of olive oil
- 2 tablespoons of bourbon
- 1/2 cup of spring onions, chopped
- 4 green garlics, chopped
- 1 red bell pepper, deveined and thinly sliced

- 1 green bell pepper, deveined and thinly sliced
- 1 tablespoon soy sauce
- 1/2 teaspoon bay leaf powder
- 1/4 teaspoon hot paprika
- 1 tablespoon honey
- 1 tablespoon Worcestershire sauce
- 2 tablespoons of ketchup

Directions

1. Set your cooker to 140 degrees F. Season the pork with salt and ground black pepper. Add to the vacuum bags.

2. Now, set the timer for 24 hours.

3. Then, preheat a large-sized stainless steel pan over a moderate flame; add the oil and swirl to coat the bottom of the pan. Once hot, sear the pork on all sides until brown crust forms. Add bourbon to deglaze the bottom of the pan.

4. Add spring onions, green garlic, bell peppers, soy sauce, bay leaf powder, hot paprika, and honey; stir to coat well.

5. Remove from the heat and add the Worcestershire sauce and ketchup. Gently stir to combine. Serve over hot couscous. Bon appétit!

51. PERFECT CHRISTMAS HAM AND PINEAPPLE KABOBS

6 Servings

Ready in about
8 hours

PER SERVING:
234 Calories; 12.6g
Fat; 17.0g Carbs; 14.2g
Protein; 10.6g Sugars

If you want to amaze your family and friends for holidays, give this recipe a try!
Serve with whole-grain mustard, tomato chutney, and sourdough buns.

Ingredients

- 1 pound of ham
- 1 teaspoon dried rosemary
- 1 teaspoon dried thyme
- 1 teaspoon dried marjoram
- 1 can of pineapple chunks, drained
- 1/2 pound of fresh mushrooms, stems removed

- 1 tablespoon honey
- 2 ½ tablespoons of rice wine vinegar
- 2 ½ tablespoons of olive oil
- 1 teaspoon garlic powder
- 1/2 teaspoon shallot powder

Directions

1. Set the cooker to 144 degrees F.

2. Cut the ham into thick slices and divide among vacuum bags. Add rosemary, thyme, and marjoram; seal the bags. Allow to sous vide for 8 hours.

3. Remove cooked ham slices from the bags and cut them into cubes. Thread ham cubes, pineapple chunks, and mushrooms onto skewers in an alternating fashion.

4. In a mixing dish, whisk the honey, vinegar, olive oil, garlic powder, and shallot powder for the basting sauce.

5. Preheat your grill and lightly grease grill grate. Brush with basting sauce frequently. Cook for about 7 minutes, turning periodically. Bon appétit!

52. PORK COUNTRY-STYLE RIBS WITH DIJON SAUCE

6 Servings

Ready in about
12 hours

PER SERVING:
290 Calories; 16.3g Fat;
2.9g Carbs; 31.8g Protein;
0.0g Sugars

These sous vide pork ribs are tender and a little slippery. In this recipe, we call for it to be cooked at 131 degrees F. If you increase the temperature of the water bath, you will get a little dry and stringy meat.

Ingredients

- 1 ½ pounds of pork country-style ribs
- 1 teaspoon kosher salt
- 1/2 teaspoon mixed peppercorns, freshly cracked
- 1/4 tablespoon ancho chili powder

- 2 thyme sprigs, finely chopped
- 3 tablespoons of Dijon mustard
- 1 ½ cups of crème fraiche

Directions

1. Set your device to cook at 131 degrees F.

2. Season the pork ribs with salt, peppercorns, ancho chili powder and thyme. Add to sous vide pouches and seal them.

3. Allow to sous vide for 10 to 12 hours. Take the pork ribs out of the water bath and remove them from the pouches.

4. Right before the sous vide pork is done, make the sauce by mixing Dijon mustard with crème fraiche; mix well to combine.

5. Pat the sous vide pork dry with a paper towel and place in a roasting pan. Roast the pork in the preheated oven at 400 degrees F for about 10 minutes, turning once or twice.

6. Serve warm with Dijon sauce on the side. Bon appétit!

53. Spicy Pepper and Pork Soup

8 Servings

Ready in about
3 hours 20 minutes

PER SERVING:
211 Calories; 12.9g Fat;
9.6g Carbs; 14.1g Protein;
3.5g Sugars

> Habanero pepper has a hint of heat so it works well in most kinds of pork soups.
> You can use a different combo of seasonings to make the most delicious soup ever!

Ingredients

- 4 pork chops
- 1/2 teaspoon kosher salt
- 1/2 teaspoon ground black pepper, or more to taste
- 1/4 teaspoon Hungarian paprika
- 1 tablespoon grapeseed oil
- 1 cup shallots, chopped
- 2 carrots, chopped
- 1 zucchini, chopped

- 1 red bell pepper, deveined and chopped
- 1 green bell pepper, deveined and chopped
- 1 Habanero pepper, deveined and chopped
- 6 cups of chicken broth
- 1 bay leaf
- 1 teaspoon cumin powder
- 1/2 teaspoon porcini powder
- 1 tablespoon Worcester sauce

Directions

1. Set the cooking machine to 135 degrees F. Season the pork chops with salt, pepper, and paprika. Throw the seasoned pork chops into the sous vide pouches.

2. Allow them to sous vide for 3 hours. Remove from the pouches and cut into cubes.

3. In an 8-quart soup pot, heat the oil over a moderate flame. Now, sauté the vegetables, including Habanero pepper until just tender and aromatic.

4. Afterwards, add the broth, bay leaf, cumin powder, and porcini powder; bring to a boil. Then, turn the heat to a simmer and cook an additional 15 minutes.

5. Drizzle with Worcester sauce. Serve hot with egg noodles if desired.

54. GRILLED PORK BACK RIBS

8 Servings

Ready in about
12 hours

PER SERVING:
331 Calories; 8.0g Fat;
1.5g Carbs; 59.6g Protein;
0.0g Sugars

In this recipe, we call for pork ribs to be cooked at 140 degrees F. Meat is meltingly tender. However, if you tend to achieve chewiness while still tenderizing a majority of the meat, use 155 degrees F; actually, it's traditional doneness temperature. It's up to you!

Ingredients

- 4 pounds of pork back ribs
- 2 tablespoons of sea salt flakes
- 1 teaspoon freshly ground black pepper
- 1 tablespoon dried parsley flakes
- 1 teaspoon cayenne pepper

- 1 tablespoon onion powder
- 1 tablespoon brown mustard
- 4 garlic cloves, peeled and sliced
- Barbecue sauce, for basting

Directions

1. Season pork back ribs with the salt flakes, black pepper, parsley flakes, cayenne pepper, and onion powder.

2. Then, rub them with mustard and slivered garlic on all sides.

3. Set your machine to 140 degrees F.

4. Transfer the pork ribs to sous vide pouches; seal them. Place in the water bath for 10 to 12 hours. Take the pouches out of the water bath. Pat the ribs dry with a dish cloth or paper towel.

5. Preheat a grill to very hot. Brush your ribs with barbecue sauce and grill for 1 minute on each side. Serve with some extra barbecue sauce.

55. Gourmet Sausages with White Wine

8 Servings

Ready in about
3 hours 10 minutes

PER SERVING:
412 Calories; 34.7g Fat;
0.4g Carbs; 22.1g Protein;
0.0g Sugars

Wine and seasonings help infuse the sausages with even more moisture and flavor than they normally have. Serve with fresh rolls, potato quesadilla or cheddar cheese. Enjoy!

Ingredients

- 2 pounds of raw pork sausages
- 1 teaspoon anchovy paste
- 1 tablespoon white wine vinegar
- 4 ounces of dry white wine
- 2 sprigs of fresh thyme, chopped
- 2 sprigs of fresh rosemary, chopped
- 1 tablespoon lard

Directions

1. Set your device to 150 degrees F.

2. Throw the sausages into sous vide pouches; add anchovy paste, vinegar, wine, thyme, and rosemary; seal the sous vide pouches.

3. Allow to sous vide for about 3 hours. Remove the sausages from the pouches and pat them dry with a dish cloth.

4. Next, add the lard in the pan that is preheated over a moderate flame. Once hot, cook your sausages for 2 to 3 minutes on each side. Bon appétit!

56. PULLED PORK TAGLIATELLE

10 Servings

Ready in about
24 hours

PER SERVING:
482 Calories; 8.7g Fat;
50.2g Carbs; 47.7g
Protein; 0.0g Sugars

Tagliatelle is one of the jewels of Italian cuisine. You can choose your own combo of seasonings just like Italian "nonna

Ingredients

- 1 tablespoon salt
- 1/2 teaspoon ground black pepper, or more to taste
- 1 teaspoon smoked cayenne pepper
- 1 teaspoon chopped fresh rosemary leaves
- 1 teaspoon shallot powder
- 1 teaspoon porcini powder
- 1 teaspoon celery seeds
- 1 teaspoon fennel seeds
- 1 teaspoon dried oregano
- 1 ½ teaspoons of dried basil
- 1/4 cup of tamari sauce
- 3 pounds of pork shoulder, excess fat removed
- 2 pounds fresh tagliatelle
- 1/2 cup pf Parmigiano-Reggiano, freshly grated

Directions

1. Set your cooker to 135 degrees F.

2. Then, thoroughly combine all the seasonings. Add tamari sauce and mix until everything is well incorporated.

3. Coat the pork shoulder with the seasoning mixture. Add to sous vide pouches; seal the pouches. Allow to sous vide for 24 hours. Shred the meat with two forks.

4. Add cooking liquids to a saucepan and simmer over medium heat until the sauce has thickened. Add the sauce to the pulled pork and stir to combine well.

5. Finally, cook tagliatelle in a lightly-salted water as directed on package. Drain tagliatelle thoroughly.

6. Serve the pulled pork over hot tagliatelle. Top with Parmigiano-Reggiano. Bon appétit!

57. PORK MEATLOAF WITH MUSHROOMS AND BACON

8 Servings

Ready in about
3 hours 15 minutes

PER SERVING:
289 Calories; 13.5g Fat;
4.0g Carbs; 36.5g Protein;
2.1g Sugars

Forget the dried-out meatloaf you may have endured in the past! Make this family
favorite even better by topping it with high-quality bacon.

Ingredients

- 2 ½ tablespoons of butter
- 1 cup of scallions, chopped
- 2 garlic cloves, peeled and minced
- 1 sweet pepper, deveined and chopped
- 1 chipotle pepper, deveined and chopped
- 1 cup of button mushrooms, stalks removed and chopped
- 2 eggs plus 1 egg white

- 1/3 cup of plain milk
- 1 tablespoon tamari sauce
- 1 tablespoon champagne vinegar
- 2 pounds of ground pork
- Salt and ground black pepper, to your liking
- 1 teaspoon smoked cayenne pepper
- 1 teaspoon minced rosemary
- 4 strips of thick-sliced bacon, cut into halves

Directions

1. Set your cooking machine to 142 degrees F.

2. Melt the butter in your saucepan that is preheated over a moderate heat; now, sauté the scallions until just fragrant.

3. Now, stir in the garlic and cook until aromatic or about 30 seconds. Stir in the peppers and mushrooms; continue sautéing for about 3 minutes.

4. Then, whisk the eggs and egg white; add the milk, tamari sauce, pork, salt, black pepper, cayenne pepper, and rosemary.

5. Shape into two meatloaves and place them in sous vide pouches. Now, submerge the pouches in the water bath. Cook for 3 hours.

6. Remove your meatloaves from the pouches and pat the surfaces dry. Now, lay bacon slices over the loaf, tucking the ends in.

7. Bake until an instant-read thermometer inserted in the meatloaves registers 150 degrees F. Allow to cool for 15 minutes before slicing and serving.

58. PORK SIRLOIN CHOPS WITH HORSERADISH SAUCE

4 Servings

Ready in about
6 hours

PER SERVING:
302 Calories; 16.0g Fat;
5.5g Carbs; 31.8g Protein;
1.3g Sugars

Relax and look forward to the incredible pork main course ahead! By using sous vide cooking method, pork remains succulent and so flavorful that all you need is a dollop of simple horseradish sauce to make it shine.

Ingredients

- 1/3 cup of tamari sauce
- 2 tablespoons of dry vermouth
- 2 tablespoons of peanut oil
- 1 teaspoon Hungarian paprika
- A pinch of ground allspice
- 1 tablespoon lemon zest, grated
- 1 ½ teaspoons of celery seeds

- 1 pound of pork sirloin chops
- Flaky sea salt and freshly ground black pepper, to taste

For the Horseradish Sauce:

- 1 tablespoon horseradish
- 1 teaspoon rice wine vinegar
- 2 tablespoons of mayonnaise
- 4 tablespoons of sour cream

Directions

1. To make the marinade, in a mixing dish, combine the tamari sauce, dry vermouth, peanut oil, Hungarian paprika, allspice, lemon zest, and celery seeds.

2. Then, season liberally the pork sirloin chops with salt and black pepper on all sides. Place in the marinade; let it marinate overnight. Take the chops out of the marinade and transfer to sous vide bags and vacuum-pack.

3. Set your cooking machine to 140 degrees F. Allow to sous vide for 6 hours. To finish, sear the pork in the preheated skillet until well browned on all sides.

4. In the meantime, make the sauce by whisking all sauce ingredients; keep in your refrigerator until ready to serve. Serve with warm pork sirloin chops and enjoy!

59. Pork Blade Steak in Garlic Sauce

4 Servings

Ready in about
20 hours

PER SERVING:
260 Calories; 10.2g Fat;
2.5g Carbs; 37.5g Protein;
0.0g Sugars

Cooking pork blade steak sous vide has a number of advantages to the traditional methods of searing or grilling. See it for yourself!

Ingredients

- 1 ¼ pounds of pork blade steak
- 1 teaspoon sea salt flakes
- 1/2 teaspoon freshly cracked mixed peppercorns
- 1/2 teaspoon smoked cayenne pepper
- 1 ½ tablespoons of grapeseed oil

- 4 garlic cloves, pressed
- 1 tablespoon all-purpose flour
- 1/4 cup of white veal stock
- 1 tablespoon fresh coriander leaves, finely minced

Directions

1. Firstly, set your cooker to 140 degrees F.

2. Season the pork blade steak with salt, cracked peppercorns, and smoked cayenne pepper. Now, place it in sous vide pouches and vacuum seal.

3. Allow it to sous vide for 20 hours.

4. Next, heat grapeseed oil in a sauté pan that is preheated over a moderate flame. Give your pork a quick sear on both sides; reserve, keeping it warm.

5. After that, add the garlic and cook in the pan drippings until just aromatic and browned; add the flour and stir.

6. Pour in veal stock and stir until the sauce has thickened and heated through. Remove from the stove and add fresh coriander leaves. Add the pork back to your pan and serve immediately.

60. MUST-SERVE SPICY PORK STEW

8 Servings

Ready in about
26 hours

PER SERVING:
264 Calories; 11.4g
Fat; 12.8g Carbs; 27.5g
Protein; 7.6g Sugars

You're about to cook the best pork stew you've ever eaten! The recipe calls for ancho chile that is actually a dried version of poblano pepper. They can be soaked in water or crushed.

Ingredients

- 1 ½ tablespoons of peanut oil
- 1 ½ pounds of pork stew meat, cubed
- 1 teaspoon sea salt flakes
- 1/4 teaspoon freshly ground black pepper, or more to taste
- 1 teaspoon cayenne pepper
- 2 medium-sized onions, peeled and chopped
- 4 garlic cloves, minced
- 1/2 pound of carrots, cut crosswise into 2-inch lengths

- 2 ancho chilies, deveined and crushed
- 1 sweet pepper, deveined and chopped
- 1 teaspoon rosemary, chopped
- 1 teaspoon dried marjoram
- A pinch of ground cloves
- 1/4 fresh lemon juice
- 3 tablespoons of champagne vinegar
- 6 plum tomatoes, quartered lengthwise
- 2 tablespoons of soy sauce
- 5 cups of chicken stock

Directions

1. Set your cooker to 140 degrees F.

2. Warm peanut oil in a stock pot over a medium-high flame. Sprinkle the pork with salt, black pepper, and cayenne pepper on all sides.

3. Cook in the hot oil, stirring periodically, until no longer pink; divide among the sous vide bags.

4. In the same pot, sauté the onions over a moderate flame. Then, stir in the garlic, carrots, ancho chilies, and sweet pepper; cook until they have softened. Add the remaining ingredients and stir.

5. Allow the pork meat to sous vide for 26 hours. Once the cooking is complete, remove the bags from the water bath. Transfer to the pot and bring to a rapid boil.

6. Cook until heated through and serve warm over cooked rice. Bon appétit!

61. PARTY BACON-INSPIRED COCKTAIL

12 Servings

Ready in about
45 minutes
+ chilling time

PER SERVING:
287 Calories; 9.9g Fat;
2.4g Carbs; 8.8g Protein;
2.1g Sugars

You can play around with the ratio to make this recipe more or less bacon-flavored; actually, bacon gives smokiness and richness to your drink.

Ingredients

For the Bacon-Infused Whiskey:

- 10 ounces of smoked bacon, cut into thick strips
- 2 ½ cups of whiskey

For the Cocktail:

- 1/2 ounce of bitters
- A splash of water
- 2 Amarena cherries in syrup
- Brown sugar, to taste
- 1 slice of lemon

Directions

1. Start by preheating your oven to 395 degrees F. Set your cooker to 155 degrees F.

2. Bake the bacon for 15 to 17 minutes. Reserve 3 ½ tablespoons of bacon grease.

3. Add the bacon to a vacuum seal bag. Add the whiskey and reserved bacon grease. Allow to sous vide for 45 minutes.

4. Now, strain the liquid through a fine-mesh sieve into a bowl. Chill for about 4 hours; after that, discard as much fat as possible.

5. Pour it through the wire-mesh strainer lined with a coffee filter into a bowl. Store at room temperature for up to 6 months or use immediately to prepare bacon-inspired cocktail.

6. For one person, you will need 2 to 2 ½ ounces of bacon-infused whiskey. Mix it with the bitters, water, and cherries.

7. Add brown sugar to a small tray. Now, dip the top of the wet glass into the brown sugar. Pour in your drink and decorate with the lemon slice. Cheers!

62. SPAGHETTI WITH RICH PORK RAGÙ

6 Servings

Ready in about
4 hours

PER SERVING:
251 Calories; 9.3g Fat;
9.4g Carbs; 31.6g Protein;
2.9g Sugars

A long-simmered meat ragù with spaghetti is a classic Italian recipe you
must try. Sous vide is one of the best cooking methods to achieve flavors that
will blow you away!

Ingredients

- 2 tablespoons of grapeseed oil
- 1 cup shallots, chopped
- 2 garlic cloves, minced
- 2 carrots, chopped
- 1 Roma tomato, chopped
- 1 cup of roasted vegetable stock
- 1/2 cup of whole milk

- 1 ½ pounds of ground pork
- 1 teaspoon flaky sea salt
- 1/2 teaspoon ground black pepper
- 1/2 teaspoon red pepper flakes, crushed
- A dash of grated nutmeg
- 1 sprig of rosemary, minced
- 1 sprig of oregano, minced

Directions

1. In a deep pan, heat the oil over a moderate flame; now, sauté the shallots, garlic, and carrot, about 8 minutes or until they have softened.

2. Stir in chopped tomato; continue sautéing for an additional 1 to 1 ½ minutes, stirring frequently.

3. Now, decrease the heat. Add the rest of the above ingredients and simmer until heated through.

4. Set the cooker to 131 degrees F. Next, add the mixture to a sous vide bag and cook for 4 hours.

5. Using tongs, remove your bags of ground meat mixture from the water bath.

6. Cook the spaghetti in a large pot of boiling salted water, stirring occasionally, until al dente. Drain and serve immediately with warm sauce.

63. CHEESE-STUFFED PORK MEATBALLS

8 Servings

Ready in about
3 hours

PER SERVING:
141 Calories; 6.8g Fat;
0.5g Carbs; 18.5g Protein;
0.0g Sugars

A twist on an old party favorite! You will want these kid-friendly, gooey meatballs for your next cocktail party or game day. Serve with cocktail picks and a sauce for dipping.

Ingredients

- 1 pound of ground pork meat
- 1 teaspoon garlic, finely minced
- 1/2 cup of fine breadcrumbs
- 1 teaspoon sea salt flakes
- 1/2 teaspoon ground black pepper, or more to taste

- 1 teaspoon dried parsley flakes
- 1 teaspoon celery seeds
- 1/2 teaspoon mustard seeds
- 1 teaspoon shallot powder
- 4 string cheese packets, cut into 1-inch cubes

Directions

1. Set your cooker to 140 degrees F.

2. Next, thoroughly combine ground pork meat with garlic and breadcrumbs. Add the seasonings and knead with oiled hands.

3. Scoop the mixture into small balls; press 1 cube of cheese into the center, sealing meat tightly around it. Repeat with remaining ingredients.

4. Carefully, place the meatballs in a single layer in the sous vide pouches. Allow them to sous vide for 3 hours.

5. Afterward, sear the meatballs in the preheated skillet, moving them around, until they're browned on all sides. Bon appétit!

64. GRILLED PORK SOUVLAKI

8 Servings

Ready in about
3 hours 40 minutes

PER SERVING:
349 Calories; 22.3g Fat;
4.3g Carbs; 31.8g Protein;
2.2g Sugars

A simple way to make souvlaki for summer grilling; you can add your favorite combo of vegetables. Great with creamy, rich salad.

Ingredients

- 2 pounds of boneless pork loin, cut into 1-inch cubes
- Fine sea salt and freshly cracked black peppercorns, to taste
- 3 garlic cloves, crushed
- 1 lemon, juiced
- 1/4 cup of olive oil

- 2 tablespoons of soy sauce
- 1/2 teaspoon cumin powder
- 1/2 teaspoon mustard powder
- 1 yellow onion, diced
- 2 sweet peppers, diced

Directions

1. Firstly, set your cooker to 140 degrees F.

2. Season the pork cubes liberally with salt and freshly cracked black peppercorns; transfer to the sous vide bags.

3. Now, add the garlic, lemon juice, olive oil, soy sauce, cumin, and mustard powder to the bags. Seal the bags and lower them into the water bath; adjust the timer to 3 hours 30 minutes.

4. Lightly oil a grill. Preheat the grill for medium-high heat. Thread pork, yellow onions, and sweet peppers onto skewers.

5. Grill approximately 10 minutes, or to the desired doneness, turning skewers frequently for even grilling. Bon appétit!

65. FAMOUS PORK BABY BACK RIBS

6 Servings

Ready in about
10 hours

PER SERVING:
268 Calories; 4.8g Fat;
24.6g Carbs; 31.1g
Protein; 21.8g Sugars

If you're looking for classic BBQ back ribs that are easy to make, look no further!
Now, you can have restaurant-style pork ribs at your own home. If you prefer
traditional, crisp roasted pork, allow it to sous vide for 20 hours at 155 degrees F.

Ingredients

- 1 ½ pounds of pork baby back ribs, cut into sections

For the Spice mix:

- 1 tablespoon sea salt flakes
- 1 teaspoon freshly cracked mixed peppercorns
- 1 tablespoon Hungarian paprika
- 1 ½ teaspoons of mustard seeds
- 1 tablespoon cumin
- 1 tablespoon chipotle powder
- 1 teaspoon dried basil

- 1 teaspoon dried oregano
- 1 ½ teaspoons of garlic powder
- 1 ½ teaspoons of shallot powder

For the Sauce:

- 1/2 cup of brown sugar
- 1/2 cup of red wine vinegar
- 1 cup of ketchup
- 1 tablespoon Worcestershire sauce
- 1 teaspoon kosher salt
- A dash of hot pepper sauce

Directions

1. Set your cooking machine to 140 degrees F. Thoroughly combine all ingredients for the spice mix.

2. Rub your pork with the spice mix and transfer to sous vide pouches. Once the sous vide water bath has reached the target temperature, lower the pouches into the preheated water bath.

3. Allow to sous vide for 10 hours.

4. Preheat a grill to very hot. Quickly grill the ribs until nicely browned on all sides.

5. In the meantime, prepare the sauce by mixing all the sauce items in your blender or food processor. Serve with hot baby back ribs. Bon appétit!

BEEF

66. MELT-IN-YOUR-MOUTH BEEF CHOPS

4 Servings

Ready in about
3 hours 20 minutes

PER SERVING:
290 Calories; 15.6g Fat;
0.9g Carbs; 34.6g Protein;
0.0g Sugars

Sous vide ensures you get moist and tender beef chops without losing any nutrition and flavor from the meat. Mound fresh salad on a plate. Top with warm beef chops and serve with your favorite side dishes.

Ingredients

- 1 pound of beef chops
- 1 teaspoon kosher salt
- 1/2 teaspoon freshly cracked black pepper
- 1 teaspoon garlic powder
- 1 teaspoon shallot powder

- 1 teaspoon ancho chili powder
- 1 bay leaf
- 1 tablespoon dried marjoram
- 2 ½ tablespoons of grapeseed oil

Directions

1. Set your cooker to 134 degrees F. Season the beef chops with salt, pepper, garlic powder, shallot powder, and ancho chili powder.

2. Transfer your chops to sous vide pouches. Lower the pouches into the preheated water bath. Then, add the bay leaf, marjoram, and grapeseed oil. Allow to sous vide for 3 hours.

3. Remove the pouches from the water bath.

4. Roast in the preheated oven around 20 minutes, turning halfway. Serve over mashed potatoes. Bon appétit!

67. Roast Sirloin with Celery-Walnut Salad

4 Servings

Ready in about
6 hours

PER SERVING:
355 Calories; 21.7g Fat;
2.5g Carbs; 36.7g Protein;
0.6g Sugars

You can't go wrong with slowly cooked and well-seasoned beef. This sirloin beef joint is cooked gently for 6 hours and then, quickly seared in hot butter; it has very rich flavor and perfectly tender, marble texture.

Ingredients

- 1 pound of sirloin beef joint
- 1 teaspoon sea salt flakes
- 1/2 teaspoon black pepper, preferably freshly ground
- 1 teaspoon red pepper flakes, crushed
- 2 tablespoons of peanut oil
- 1 teaspoon dried rosemary
- 1 teaspoon dried thyme
- 2 bay leaves

- 1 tablespoon softened butter

For the Celery-Walnut Salad:

- 1/4 cup of walnuts, toasted and roughly chopped
- 4 celery stalks, thinly sliced
- 2 tablespoons of fresh lemon juice
- 1 tablespoon champagne vinegar
- 1 teaspoon cumin seeds
- 2 tablespoons of extra-virgin olive oil

Directions

1. Set your cooker to 136 degrees F.

2. Season the beef with salt, black pepper, and red pepper. Add to the sous vide bags; divide the peanut oil, rosemary, thyme, and bay leaves among the bags and vacuum-pack.

3. Allow to sous vide for 6 hours.

4. Melt the butter over a moderate flame; once hot, sear the beef on all sides, flipping once or twice, until it is richly browned.

5. In the meantime, prepare the salad by tossing all salad items in a large bowl. Keep in your fridge until ready to serve. Serve as accompaniment alongside your beef. Bon appétit!

68. Yogurt and Garam Masala Rib Eye

4 Servings

Ready in about
2 hours

PER SERVING:
228 Calories; 10.8g Fat;
3.3g Carbs; 28.0g Protein;
2.9g Sugars

A well-prepared ribeye steak is a royal meal. Cooking it sous vide before searing in hot oil ensures your beef stays tender and flavorful.

Ingredients

- 1 (3/4-pound) of ribeye steak
- 1 teaspoon sea salt flakes
- 1/2 teaspoon ground black pepper
- 1 teaspoon cayenne pepper
- 1 teaspoon ground coriander
- 1/4 teaspoon ground cumin
- 1 tablespoon peanut oil, for frying
- 1 teaspoon garam masala
- 1 cup of natural yoghurt

Directions

1. Set your cooking machine to 158 degrees F. Rinse the meat and pat it dry.

2. Then, sprinkle your ribeye with salt flakes, black pepper, cayenne pepper, coriander, and cumin. Place in a sous vide bag and vacuum seal; lower into the preheated water bath.

3. Set the timer for 2 hours. Remove the meat from the pouch and pat dry.

4. Then, add the oil to a heavy skillet to cover the bottom. Sear the beef on all sides until it's nicely browned, approximately 1 minute per side.

5. Add the garam masala and yogurt and continue cooking until heated through. Serve immediately and enjoy!

69. JUICY HERBED FLANK STEAK

6 Servings

Ready in about
8 hours 15 minutes
+ marinating time

PER SERVING:
254 Calories; 10.9g Fat;
1.6g Carbs; 35.4g Protein;
0.6g Sugars

Beef is a staple for most meat lovers, from meatballs to the Christmas roast. Try something new and amaze your family and friends with this juicy and flavorsome flank steak!

Ingredients

- 1 ½ pounds of flank steak, cut it into 4 long strips
- Salt and black pepper, to taste

For the Marinade:

- 2 tablespoons of lemon juice
- 1 ½ tablespoons of extra-virgin olive oil
- 2 garlic cloves, crushed
- 1 teaspoon chili powder

For the Steak:

- 1 egg white, well beaten
- 1/2 teaspoon curry powder
- 1/2 teaspoon cayenne pepper
- 1/2 teaspoon dried thyme
- 1 teaspoon dried rosemary
- 1 teaspoon dried parsley flakes
- 1 teaspoon mustard seeds
- 1 teaspoon granulated garlic

Directions

1. Set the cooker to 140 degrees F. Generously salt and pepper flank steak. Mix all ingredients for the marinade in a large bowl.

2. Add the steak, cover and place it in the fridge for at least 1 hour.

3. Then, transfer the meat to sous vide pouches. Cook for 8 hours. Remove the steak pieces from the pouches and dip them in egg white.

4. Now, combine thoroughly the remaining seasonings. Rub the meat with the spice mix. Broil the steak for about 5 minutes per side. Check the steak for doneness and serve with boiled potatoes. Bon appétit!

70. Beef Brisket with Chili-Peanut Sauce

6 Servings

Ready in about
48 hours

PER SERVING:
312 Calories; 14.8g Fat;
5.7g Carbs; 38.6g Protein;
3.0g Sugars

Fork tender meat with a perfectly chewy texture. These beef briskets need just a quick sear to gain a nice crust and amazing taste. Serve with pasta or mashed sweet potatoes.

Ingredients

- 1 ½ pounds of beef brisket, cut into pieces
- Sea salt and freshly ground black pepper, to taste
- 1 teaspoon red pepper flakes, crushed
- 1 teaspoon garlic powder
- 1 teaspoon onion powder
- 1/2 teaspoon bay leaf powder
- 1/3 cup of peanut butter
- 1 teaspoon sugar
- 1 ½ tablespoons of tamari sauce
- 1 tablespoon chili paste

Directions

1. Set your cooking machine to 140 degrees F.

2. Season the beef brisket with salt, black pepper, red pepper, garlic powder, onion powder, and bay leaf powder.

3. Add the beef brisket to the sous vide bags. Lower them into the water bath and cook for 48 hours.

4. In the meantime, whisk the peanut butter, sugar, tamari sauce, and chili paste until everything is well incorporated.

5. Afterwards, sear the beef in the preheated skillet until it has reached a medium brown color. Add the chili-peanut sauce and stir until heated through.

6. Serve right away with your favorite side dish.

71. COUNTRY-STYLE BEEF AND BEER STEW

8 Servings

Ready in about
6 hours

PER SERVING:
220 Calories; 8.1g Fat;
6.4g Carbs; 27.2g Protein;
1.9g Sugars

Indulge in this sous vide comforting beef stew which is perfect for chilly winter days. Serve with steamed green beans and homemade crusty bread.

Ingredients

- 1 ½ pounds of beef stew meat, cubed
- 1 ½ tablespoons of olive oil
- 1 shallot, chopped
- 1 celery stalk with leaves, chopped
- 1 carrot, trimmed and chopped
- 1 parsnip, trimmed and chopped
- 1 red bell pepper, deveined and chopped
- 1 green bell pepper, deveined and chopped

- 1 jalapeño pepper, deveined and chopped
- 2 garlic cloves, chopped
- 2 tablespoons of cornstarch
- 1 cup of lager beer
- 2 cups of beef stock
- 1 tablespoon soy sauce
- 1 teaspoon dried marjoram
- Chopped fresh cilantro leaves, for garnish

Directions

1. Set your cooker to 136 degrees F. Pat the stew meat dry with a dish cloth.

2. Add olive oil to a deep saucepan that is preheated over a moderate flame. Brown the meat for about 7 minutes, stirring periodically.

3. Next, stir in the shallot, celery, carrot, parsnip, and peppers; sauté for 3 to 5 more minutes. Add the garlic and cornstarch, and cook another 1 minute or until just aromatic.

4. Add beer to deglaze the pan. Add 1 cup of stock, soy sauce, and marjoram. Bring to a rapid boil; then, turn the heat to medium. Simmer until your sauce has thickened slightly.

5. Add the mixture to your sous vide bags; lower the bags into the preheated water and cook for 5 hours 30 minutes.

6. Pour the accumulated cooking juices through a fine-mesh sieve into the pot; add remaining 1 cup of stock and bring to a rolling boil; turn the heat to a simmer.

7. Continue cooking at a lively simmer, whisking periodically, until the broth is completely smooth.

8. Add the reserved ingredients and serve warm topped with fresh cilantro. Bon appétit!

72. Beef Steak Fajitas

4 Servings

Ready in about
1 hour

PER SERVING:
485 Calories; 17.1g Fat;
5.5g Carbs; 73.6g Protein;
3.1g Sugars

You can buy ready-made fajita seasoning or make your own. Serve steak fajitas with tortillas, mayonnaise, guacamole, and salsa.

Ingredients

For the Fajita Seasoning:

- 1 teaspoon chili powder
- 1 teaspoon salt
- 1 teaspoon paprika
- 1 teaspoon brown sugar
- 1/2 teaspoon garlic powder
- 1/2 teaspoon onion powder

For the Beef Steak Fajitas:

- 4 fillet mignon steaks
- 2 tablespoons of grapeseed oil
- 2 garlic cloves, chopped
- 1 shallot, chopped
- 1 red bell pepper, deveined and chopped
- 1 green bell pepper, deveined and chopped
- 1/4 cup of vermouth
- 1/3 cup of vegetable broth
- 1 tablespoon soy sauce

Directions

1. Set your cooker to 135 degrees F. Rinse the meat and pat dry.

2. Mix all ingredients for the fajita seasoning. Then, season the fillet mignon with prepared fajita seasoning.

3. Divide the meat among the sous vide bags. Vacuum seal in separate pouches and arrange the pouches in a rack to separate them in the water bath.

4. Allow to sous vide for 50 minutes.

5. While the fillet mignons are cooking, heat 2 tablespoons of grapeseed oil in a frying pan over medium-high flame.

6. Sauté the garlic, shallot, and peppers until just tender and aromatic. Add the vermouth to scrape up any browned bits from the bottom of your pan.

7. Pour in the broth and bring to a rolling boil; turn the heat to a simmer. Let it simmer until the liquid has thickened.

8. Remove from the heat and add soy sauce. Transfer the sautéed vegetables to a bowl and keep them warm.

9. Raise the heat; sear the steak in the same pan for 1 to 2 minutes per side. Serve the fillet mignon steaks on individual plates with sautéed vegetables.

73. SUMMER SPICY PEPPERY BEEF SALAD

4 Servings

Ready in about
12 hours

PER SERVING:
272 Calories; 11.6g
Fat; 14.0g Carbs; 28.0g
Protein; 7.8g Sugars

This rich and nutritious main-course salad combines lemony-flavored dressing with refreshing tomatoes, sautéed vegetables and grilled steak. Enjoy!

Ingredients

- 3/4 pound of skirt steak
- 1 teaspoon salt
- 1/2 teaspoon ground black pepper, or more to taste
- 1/3 teaspoon cayenne pepper
- 3/4 tablespoon lard
- 1 jalapeño pepper, deveined and chopped
- 1 sweet pepper, deveined and chopped
- 1 celery stalk with leaves, trimmed and chopped
- 1 large-sized carrot, trimmed and chopped

- 2 parsnips, trimmed and chopped
- 1/2 cup of minced shallots
- 1 teaspoon granulated garlic
- 1 pound of grape tomatoes, quartered
- 1 tablespoon fresh lemon juice
- 1 tablespoon cider vinegar
- 1 tablespoon palm sugar
- 1 tablespoon soy sauce
- 1 tablespoon olive oil
- Toasted sesame seeds, for garnish
- Fresh, chopped chives, for garnish

Directions

1. Firstly, pat skirt steak dry with a clean kitchen towel. Generously season with salt, black pepper, and cayenne pepper.

2. Set the cooking machine to 135 degrees F. Transfer the meat to sous vide bags and vacuum seal. Allow to sous vide for 10 to 12 hours. Remove the meat from the bags; pat them dry.

3. Preheat a barbecue grill on high. Now, grill skirt steak for 3 minutes per side. Thinly slice steak across the grain and transfer to a salad bowl.

4. Then, melt the lard in a saucepan that is preheated over a moderate heat. Now, sauté the peppers, celery, carrot, parsnip, and shallots until just tender. Add granulated garlic and stir for another 1 minute.

5. Allow them to cool slightly and transfer to the salad bowl with sliced skirt steak. Then, add tomatoes and toss to combine.

6. In a small mixing dish, thoroughly whisk the lemon juice, vinegar, palm sugar, soy sauce, and olive oil. Drizzle the dressing over the salad and serve garnished with toasted sesame seeds and fresh chives. Bon appétit!

74. Rump Roast with Mustard-Butter Sauce

6 Servings

Ready in about
50 minutes

PER SERVING:
301 Calories; 17.4g Fat;
2.1g Carbs; 34.6g Protein;
0.0g Sugars

Is there anything better than rich warm soup with fresh noodles? If you like a piquant flavor, drizzle each serving with the chili oil.

Ingredients

- 1 ½ pounds of rump steak
- 1 teaspoon sea salt
- 1/2 teaspoon pink peppercorns, freshly cracked
- 1 teaspoon cumin powder
- 1/2 teaspoon onion powder

- 1 teaspoon dried parsley flakes
- 1 tablespoon rendered bacon fat
- 1/4 cup of butter, room temperature
- 1 ½ tablespoons of whole-grain mustard
- 1 teaspoon garlic, minced
- 1/3 teaspoon anchovy paste

Directions

1. Set your cooking machine between 122 and 158 degrees F. Then, pat rump steak dry with a kitchen towel.

2. Sprinkle the steak with salt, cracked peppercorns, cumin powder, onion powder, and parsley flakes.

3. Add to the sous vide bags and vacuum seal. Lower the bags into the preheated water bath and cook for 45 minutes.

4. Melt the rendered bacon fat in a frying pan. Once hot, sear rump roast on all sides until well browned.

5. Meanwhile, make the sauce by mixing all sauce items. Serve with warm rump roast. Bon appétit!

75. MEATLOAF DE PROVENCE

6 Servings

Ready in about
2 hours 40 minutes

PER SERVING:
264 Calories; 9.0g Fat;
6.6g Carbs; 37.3g Protein;
2.7g Sugars

Here's a recipe for scrumptious family dinner you'll never want to be without.
Herbes de Provence mix creates a burst of flavor!

Ingredients

- 1 ½ pounds of lean ground beef
- 1 teaspoon sea salt flakes
- 1/2 teaspoon ground black pepper
- 1/2 teaspoon cayenne pepper
- 1/2 teaspoon dried parsley flakes
- 1/2 teaspoon mustard seeds
- 1/2 teaspoon chipotle powder
- 2 garlic cloves, minced

- 1 large-sized shallot, minced
- 1 tablespoon Herbes de Provence
- 1 whole egg plus 1 egg white
- 4 tablespoons of fresh breadcrumbs
- 1/3 cup of tomato sauce
- 2 tablespoons of ketchup
- 1 teaspoon dried rosemary
- 1 teaspoon brown sugar

Directions

1. Set your cooker to 135 degrees F.

2. In a mixing dish, thoroughly combine the ground beef, salt, black pepper, cayenne pepper, parsley flakes, mustard seeds, chipotle powder, garlic, minced shallot, and Herbes de Provence.

3. After that, stir in the eggs and fresh breadcrumbs. Divide the mixture into three meat loaves; carefully place each meatloaf into separate sous vide bags; vacuum seal.

4. Lower the bags into the preheated water bath; allow to sous vide for 2 hours 30 minutes.

5. Meanwhile, mix the tomato sauce, ketchup, rosemary, and brown sugar. Spread this tomato mixture to cover the entire surfaces of your meatloaves.

6. Cook in the preheated oven at 440 degrees F for 7 to 8 minutes. Afterwards, carve the meatloaves with a serrated or electric knife and serve with your favorite salad. Bon appétit!

76. The Best Burgers Ever

6 Servings

Ready in about
35 minutes

PER SERVING:
610 Calories; 24.5g
Fat; 33.7g Carbs; 60.9g
Protein; 6.5g Sugars

Ooey-gooey small burgers that are full of flavor thanks to the carefully selected seasonings. Serve with pickles and a decadent sauce of your choice.

Ingredients

- 2 pounds of ground chuck, ground
- 1 egg, lightly beaten
- 1 teaspoon kosher salt
- 1/2 teaspoon black peppercorns, freshly cracked
- 1/4 teaspoon green peppercorns, freshly cracked

- 1/2 teaspoon bay leaf powder
- 1 teaspoon garlic powder
- 12 small-sized dinner rolls
- 12 slices of American cheese

Directions

1. Firstly, mix the ground meat with egg, salt, peppercorns, bay leaf, and garlic powder.

2. Set your cooker to 140 degrees F.

3. Shape the mixture into 12 equal patties. Carefully place the patties in sous vide bags; make sure to arrange them in a single layer. Allow to sous vide for 25 minutes.

4. Serve them on dinner rolls and top each serving with a slice of American cheese. Bon appétit!

77. Beef Tenderloin Cubes in Beer-Mustard Sauce

8 Servings

Ready in about
2 hours

PER SERVING:
365 Calories; 17.2g
Fat; 16.6g Carbs; 33.8g
Protein; 13.3g Sugars

Mix a beer with the hot mustard, ketchup, chili sauce and other great ingredients for an incredibly tasty sauce. This recipe might go on your list of favorite Sunday meals

Ingredients

- 2 pounds of beef tenderloin, cubed
- 1 tablespoon whole-grain mustard
- Salt and cracked black peppercorns, to taste
- 1 teaspoon dried marjoram
- 1 tablespoon peanut oil
- 1 ½ tablespoons of softened butter

For the Sauce:

- 10 ounces of ketchup
- 1/4 cup of chili sauce
- 2 tablespoons of Worcestershire sauce
- 2 tablespoons of hot mustard
- 1/4 cup of brown sugar
- 2 tablespoons of cider vinegar
- 1 tablespoon olive oil
- 1/2 cup of beer

Directions

1. Set the cooker to 140 degrees F.

2. Toss the tenderloin cubes with the mustard. Sprinkle the tenderloin with salt, cracked peppercorns and marjoram.

3. Drizzle peanut oil over tenderloin cubes and transfer them to sous vide bags. Submerge the bags in the water bath and let simmer for 1 hour 30 minutes.

4. After that, add the butter to a cast-iron skillet that is preheated over a medium-high flame. Quickly sear the meat until nicely browned.

5. In the meantime, combine all the ingredients for the sauce in a saucepan. Let it simmer for about 13 minutes or until it has slightly thickened. Spoon over seared beef tenderloin and serve warm. Bon appétit!

78. STEAK SANDWICHES WITH CRANBERRY KETCHUP

8 Servings

Ready in about
20 hours

PER SERVING:
532 Calories; 16.5g
Fat; 33.8g Carbs; 58.6g
Protein; 3.6g Sugars

Served with cranberry ketchup and lots of fresh, crispy lettuce, these sandwiches would win your heart! Flank steak can be a little tough so you should cook it about 20 hours and slice thinly against the grain.

Ingredients

- 3 pounds of flank steak
- Salt and crushed red pepper flakes, to taste
- 1 teaspoon black pepper, preferably freshly ground
- 1 tablespoon rendered bacon fat

- 1/4 cup of ketchup
- 1/4 cup of whole berry cranberry sauce
- 8 buns
- Fresh lettuce leaves, to serve

Directions

1. Season your flank steak with salt, red pepper, and black pepper. Transfer to large sous-vide pouches.

2. Allow to sous vide at 140 degrees F for 20 hours. Remove the steak from the pouches and pat dry.

3. Melt the rendered bacon fat in a heavy skillet; heat on high until it begins to smoke; sear the steak working in batches.

4. Meanwhile, make the sauce by simply mixing the ketchup with whole berry cranberry sauce; place in the refrigerator until ready to use.

5. Cut the steak into slices and place on the bottom bun; top with the prepared sauce and lettuce leaves. Bon appétit!

79. ALL-STAR ELEGANT CHRISTMAS DINNER

8 Servings

Ready in about
10 hours

PER SERVING:
374 Calories; 16.9g Fat;
6.3g Carbs; 46.7g Protein;
1.6g Sugars

Looking for festive Christmas dinner ideas? This recipe is so addictive, that you will make it year after year. Serve over hot couscous.

Ingredients

- 3 pounds of tri-tip steak, cut into bite-sized chunks
- Sea salt and ground black pepper, to taste
- 1 teaspoon garlic powder
- 1/2 teaspoon chipotle powder
- 1/2 teaspoon porcini powder
- 1/2 teaspoon turmeric powder
- 1 teaspoon smoked cayenne pepper
- 1/2 teaspoon dried basil

- 1 teaspoon dried dill weed
- 1/4 teaspoon bay leaf powder
- 1 ½ tablespoons of grapeseed oil
- 1 ½ tablespoons of rendered bacon fat
- 1 cup of shallots, minced
- 1 cup of porcini mushrooms, chopped
- 2/3 cup of dry red wine
- 2 Roma tomatoes, seeded and chopped
- 1 tablespoon ketchup

Directions

1. Set your cooking machine to 140 degrees F.

2. Toss the beef cubes with all the seasonings. Transfer to the sous vide bags, along with the grapeseed oil; allow to sous vide for 10 hours.

3. During the last 30 minutes of cooking, preheat a heavy skillet over a medium-high heat; add rendered bacon fat.

4. Once hot, sauté the shallots until just tender and fragrant; stir in the mushrooms and continue sautéing for a few more minutes.

5. Now, pour in the wine and stir to deglaze the bottom of your skillet; turn the heat to medium-low and add chopped tomatoes and ketchup; cook, uncovered, until the sauce has reduced by half.

6. Remove the beef from the bags and add to the skillet with the mushroom sauce; allow to simmer until heated through. Bon appétit!

80. Slurp-Worthy Beef Soup with Brown Rice

4 Servings

Ready in about
12 hours

PER SERVING:
433 Calories; 15.3g
Fat; 45.4g Carbs; 28.1g
Protein; 5.0g Sugars

Consider the other add-ons such as noodles, angel hair, dumplings, or green beans. This recipe may sound fancy-schmancy but it is so easy to make by using sous vide technique. Give it a try and you will be amazed.

Ingredients

- 3/4 pounds of skirt steak
- 1 teaspoon salt
- 1/2 teaspoon ground black pepper, or more to taste
- 1/3 teaspoon red pepper flakes, crushed
- 1 ½ tablespoons of grapeseed oil
- 1 cup scallions, chopped
- 1 garlic clove, pressed
- 1 celery, chopped
- 1 medium-sized carrot, chopped
- 1 turnip, trimmed and chopped
- Salt and freshly ground black pepper, to your liking
- 1 teaspoon fresh or dried dill weed
- 1/2 teaspoon marjoram
- 1/2 teaspoon celery seeds
- 1/2 teaspoon fennel seeds
- 2 bay leaves
- 2 plum tomatoes, seeded and chopped
- 4 ½ cups of bone broth
- 1 cup of cooked brown rice

Directions

1. Firstly, pat skirt steak dry with a clean kitchen towel. Generously season with salt, black pepper, and red pepper.

2. Set the cooking machine to 135 degrees F. Transfer the meat to sous vide bags and vacuum seal. Allow to sous vide for 10 to 12 hours. Remove the meat from the bags; pat them dry.

3. Afterward, quickly sear the skirt steak on all sides. Thinly slice the steak across the grain and reserve, keeping warm.

4. In a large pot, heat the oil over a moderate flame; once hot, sauté the scallions, garlic, celery, carrot and turnip until they have softened.

5. Stir in the rest of the above ingredients, minus brown rice, bringing to a rapid boil; turn the heat to a gentle simmer. Allow your soup to simmer for approximately 13 minutes.

6. Add cooked rice and stir for a further 1 to 2 minutes or until warmed through. Serve in individual soup bowls. Bon appétit!

81. GRAPE JELLY MEATBALLS

6 Servings

Ready in about
4 hours

PER SERVING:
349 Calories; 5.1g Fat;
67.3g Carbs; 8.2g Protein;
47.0g Sugars

Meatballs are a true comfort food for any occasion. Tangy grape jelly balances an extra-hot dose of chili sauce in these tasty sumptuous meatballs.

Ingredients

- 1 ½ pounds of ground chuck
- 1/2 cup of crushed pretzels
- Plain milk to soak crushed pretzels
- 1 teaspoon salt
- 1/2 teaspoon ground black pepper
- 1 egg, whisked
- 1/2 cup onion, peeled and chopped

- 1 teaspoon minced garlic
- 1 teaspoon dried basil
- 1/2 teaspoon bay leaf powder
- 1 tablespoon shallot powder
- 20 ounces of grape jelly
- 1 (12-ounce) bottle chili sauce
- 1/2 teaspoon red pepper flakes, crushed

Directions

1. Mix the ground chuck with crushed pretzels, milk, salt, black pepper, egg, onion, minced garlic, basil, bay leaf powder, and shallot powder.

2. Shape the beef mixture into small balls; freeze them for at least 1 hour. Set the cooker to 135 degrees F.

3. Place the meatballs in sous vide pouches. Lower the pouches into the preheated water bath and cook for 3 hours.

4. In a saucepan, cook the grape jelly, chili sauce, and red pepper flakes over medium-high flame until cooked through.

5. Remove the pouches from the water bath and transfer the meatballs to the sauce. Cook until thoroughly cooked.

82. Beef Cheeks in Mushroom-Pepper Sauce

4 Servings

Ready in about
8 hours
+ marinating time

PER SERVING:
367 Calories; 13.1g Fat;
9.3g Carbs; 36.1g Protein;
4.4g Sugars

You can add any additional herbs or aromatics you like. You can also add a few strips of bacon to the mushroom mixture and skip the butter.

Ingredients

- 1 ½ cups of dry red wine
- 2 garlic cloves, smashed
- 1 rib celery, chopped
- 1 teaspoon onion powder
- A pinch of freshly grated nutmeg
- 1 teaspoon dried parsley flakes
- 1 pound of beef cheeks, cut into 4 pieces
- 1 teaspoon seasoned salt

- 1/4 teaspoon ground black pepper, or more to your liking
- 1/2 teaspoon smoked paprika
- 2 tablespoons of butter, room temperature
- 1 ¼ cups of button mushrooms, sliced
- 2 garlic cloves, crushed
- 2 sweet peppers, seeded and chopped
- Seasoned salt and white pepper, to taste

Directions

1. In a mixing dish, thoroughly combine the wine, garlic, celery, onion powder, nutmeg, and parsley flakes.

2. Season the beef cheeks with the seasoned salt, black pepper, and smoked paprika. Place in the marinade and refrigerate overnight or at least 6 hours.

3. Set the cooker to 179 degrees F.

4. Reserve the marinade and transfer the beef cheeks to sous vide pouches. Lower the pouches into the water bath; allow them to cook for 8 hours. Allow the pouches of beef to cool for 10 minutes.

5. Meanwhile, melt 1 tablespoon of butter in a heavy skillet that is preheated over a moderate flame. Now, sauté your mushrooms until tender and fragrant; stir in the garlic and peppers and continue sautéing until just tender. Season with salt and white pepper to taste and set aside keeping warm.

6. In the same skillet, melt the remaining 1 tablespoon of butter and sear the beef cheeks until nicely browned on all sides.

7. After that, add the cooking juices from the sous vide pouches along with the reserved mushroom/pepper mixture and a splash of reserved marinade. Cook until thoroughly warmed. Serve immediately. Bon appétit!

83. Barbecued Topside Beef with Vegetables

4 Servings

Ready in about
14 hours 15 minutes

PER SERVING:
327 Calories; 19.4g Fat;
2.7g Carbs; 34.7g Protein;
1.2g Sugars

Grilled beef with vegetables is a must-serve recipe during the summer months. In addition, you can grill eggplant, green onions, peppers, etc. If you're grilling beef, it's very important to massage the oil into the meat so don't skip any recipe steps.

Ingredients

- 1 pound of topside beef
- Salt and freshly cracked black peppercorns, to taste
- 2 tablespoons of extra-virgin olive oil

- 1 large-sized zucchini, sliced lengthwise
- 1 cup of purple onions, cut into thick slices
- 1 cup of Portobello mushrooms
- 1 ½ tablespoons of extra-virgin olive oil

Directions

1. Begin by seasoning the topside beef with salt and cracked black peppercorns; massage the olive oil into the beef. Seal the seasoned beef inside a vacuum bag.

2. Set your cooker to 130 degrees F. Allow it to sous vide for 14 hours.

3. Using a preheated barbeque, cook topside beef for 4 to 5 minutes per side. Drizzle the vegetables with olive oil and grill alongside your meat. Taste for doneness, adjust the seasonings and serve warm.

84. T-Bone Steak with Garlic-Parsley Sauce

4 Servings

Ready in about
2 hours 50 minutes

PER SERVING:
391 Calories; 15.4g Fat;
2.4g Carbs; 51.8g Protein;
0.9g Sugars

T-bone steak with garlicky sauce makes an impressive festive dinner. This is one of the most popular cuts of meat so you can't go wrong!

Ingredients

- 1 ½ pounds of T-bone steak, cut into 4 portions
- 1 teaspoon celery salt
- 1/4 teaspoon red pepper flakes, crushed
- 1/4 teaspoon freshly ground black pepper
- 1 teaspoon dried thyme leaves, crushed
- 1 ½ tablespoons of lard, room temperature
- 1/2 cup of purple onions, chopped

- 1 small-sized garlic head, peeled and crushed
- 1/2 cup of dry red wine
- 1 cup of bone broth
- 1 teaspoon oyster sauce
- A few dashes of tomato-based chili sauce
- 1/2 cup of packed fresh parsley leaves

Directions

1. Season the beef with celery salt, red pepper, black pepper, and thyme. Transfer to sous vide pouches.

2. Allow to sous vide in the preheated water bath at 140 degrees F for 2 hours 30 minutes. Reserve cooking liquid.

3. Heat a heavy-bottomed skillet over medium-high flame and add lard; once hot, sear the steak until nicely browned on all sides.

4. In the same skillet, cook the onion and garlic until just tender and aromatic, for about 3 minutes; make sure to stir constantly.

5. Add the remaining items, along with the reserved cooking liquid, and cook for an additional 12 to 17 minutes or until the sauce has reduced by half.

6. Return the beef pieces to the skillet and spoon the sauce over them to coat well. Bon appétit!

85. Hearty Pasta Beef Stew

6 Servings

Ready in about
1 hour 15 minutes

PER SERVING:
396 Calories; 14.9g
Fat; 15.3g Carbs; 48.5g
Protein; 4.0g Sugars

Cooking sous vide is easier than its fancy- schmancy name might sound. Try this delicious, hearty stew and enjoy chilly winter days.

Ingredients

- 2 pounds of sirloin steak, boneless and cut into bite-sized cubes
- Salt and ground black pepper, to your liking
- 1/2 teaspoon red pepper flakes, crushed
- 2 tablespoons of olive oil
- 1 cup red onions, finely chopped
- 4 garlic cloves, pressed
- 1/2 cup turnip, chopped
- 2 sweet peppers, deveined and chopped

- 1 habanero pepper, deveined and chopped
- 1 cup of button mushrooms, sliced
- 1/4 teaspoon savory
- 1/2 teaspoon bay leaf powder
- 1/2 teaspoon celery seeds
- 1 ½ cups of roasted vegetable broth
- 1 tablespoon red wine vinegar
- 1 tablespoon cornstarch
- 1 cup pasta shells

Directions

1. Firstly, toss the sirloin steak cubes with salt, black pepper, and red pepper. Add to the sous vide pouches.

2. Lower the pouches into the preheated water bath and cook at 122 degrees F for 45 minutes.

3. In the meantime, heat a large pot over a moderate flame and add the olive oil; once hot, sauté the onion until translucent.

4. Now, stir in the garlic and cook just for 30 seconds more, stirring regularly. Add the turnip, peppers, and mushrooms; season with savory, bay leaf powder, and celery seeds and cook until they have softened.

5. Next, pour in the broth and bring to a rapid boil over medium-high heat; reduce the heat to a simmer and add red wine, vinegar, and cornstarch. Let it simmer for an additional 10 minutes.

6. Add the pasta shells and cook another 20 minutes, stirring periodically. Serve immediately.

FISH & SEAFOOD

86. SPRING TROUT AND AVOCADO SALAD

6 Servings

Ready in about
35 minutes

PER SERVING:
247 Calories; 15.5g
Fat; 10.1g Carbs; 18.5g
Protein; 3.2g Sugars

This refreshing salad makes a great spring meal! You can add cherry tomato halves if desired. Serve with naan and enjoy!

Ingredients

- 6 trout fillets, skinless
- 1 teaspoon seasoned salt
- 1/2 teaspoon mixed peppercorns, freshly cracked
- 1/4 teaspoon smoked paprika
- 1 teaspoon dried thyme
- 1 teaspoon dried rosemary
- 1/2 teaspoon garlic powder

- 1 large-sized avocado, pitted and thinly sliced
- 6 scallions, sliced
- 3 cucumbers, thinly sliced
- 8 radishes, sliced
- 1 ½ tablespoons of extra-virgin olive oil
- Salt, to taste
- Lemon juice, for drizzling

Directions

1. Set the cooker to 130 degrees F. Then, rinse the trout fillets and pat them dry with a kitchen towel.

2. Season the fillets with salt, peppercorns, paprika, thyme, rosemary, and garlic powder.

3. Place them in a single layer in sous vide bags; vacuum seal. Submerge the bags in the preheated water bath; allow it to sous vide for 30 minutes. Afterwards, let them chill in your refrigerator.

4. Then, cut the fish into the strips and toss with avocado, scallions, cucumber, and radishes. Drizzle with olive oil and toss to coat well.

5. Season with salt and adjust the seasonings. Drizzle with fresh lemon juice and serve immediately.

87. Easy Flaky Salmon Steak

4 Servings

Ready in about
40 minutes

PER SERVING:
284 Calories; 13.8g Fat;
1.3g Carbs; 39.4g Protein;
0.0g Sugars

Salmon is a heart-healthy food and a pantry staple in many kitchens worldwide.
This is a great idea to include omega-3 fatty acids into your diet.

Ingredients

- 4 salmon steaks
- 1 ½ tablespoons of cider vinegar
- 1 tablespoon soy sauce
- 1 teaspoon olive oil
- 1 teaspoon capers

- 1 teaspoon cumin powder
- 1/2 teaspoon mustard powder
- 2 garlic cloves, minced
- 1 lemon, cut into wedges

Directions

1. Divide the salmon steaks among sous vide pouches. Then, divide the remaining ingredients, minus lemon wedges, among pouches.

2. Shake to distribute all ingredients evenly. Lower the pouches into the preheated water bath. Cook at 130 degrees F for 35 minutes.

3. Serve on individual serving plates garnished with fresh lemon wedges. Bon appétit!

88. BAKED CURRIED SNAPPER FILLETS

6 Servings

Ready in about
55 minutes

PER SERVING:
354 Calories; 25.7g
Fat; 19.5g Carbs; 14.1g
Protein; 0.7g Sugars

It's time to tackle a new challenge with sous vide snapper! No worries, this technique makes cooking a breeze. If you don't prefer the citrus flavor, just omit the lemon slices.

Ingredients

- 6 snapper fillets
- Celery salt and freshly cracked green peppercorns, to taste
- 1 ½ teaspoons of dried tarragon
- 1 ½ teaspoons of ground dried sage
- 3 tablespoons of olive oil

- 3 scallions, chopped
- 1 teaspoon minced garlic, chopped
- 12 slices of lemon
- 2 tablespoons of curry paste
- 2 tablespoons of peanut oil

Directions

1. Set your cooker to 130 degrees F.

2. Season snapper fillets liberally with the celery salt, green peppercorns, tarragon, and sage. Now, drizzle each fillet with olive oil.

3. After that, put the snapper fillets into 3 sous vide bags. Add 1 chopped scallion to each bag; divide the garlic among the bags; place 2 slices of lemon on each fillet. Vacuum seal and lower into the preheated water bath.

4. Allow the bags of fish fillets to sous vide for 35 minutes. Remove the fillets from the bags and pat them dry.

5. Preheat your oven to 390 degrees F. Line a baking sheet with parchment paper.

6. Thoroughly combine curry paste and peanut oil in a small mixing bowl. Spread the paste mixture over the fish and season to taste.

7. Bake snapper fillets for 12 to 15 minutes; allow them to rest for 5 to 6 minutes. Serve warm garnished with some extra lemon slices.

89. MACKEREL FILLETS WITH MACADAMIA PESTO

4 Servings

Ready in about
45 minutes

PER SERVING:
504 Calories; 45.9g Fat;
2.9g Carbs; 22.5g Protein;
0.8g Sugars

Macadamia nut is high in antioxidants, vitamins, minerals, and dietary fiber. Mackerel is a great source of omega 3 fatty acids, potassium, and very important anti-inflammatory compounds. Serve accompanied by dry white wine.

Ingredients

- 4 mackerel fillets, pin boned
- Seasoned salt and crushed red pepper flakes, to taste
- 1 teaspoon minced coriander
- 1 teaspoon dried parsley flakes
- 2 tablespoons of olive oil

For the Macadamia Pesto:

- 1/2 cup of toasted macadamia nuts
- 2 tablespoons of fresh basil leaves
- 2 tablespoons of fresh mint leaves
- 1 garlic clove, minced
- Juiced and grated rind of 1 lemon
- 3 tablespoons of olive oil
- Water, as needed

Directions

1. Set your cooker to 128 degrees F.

2. Season mackerel fillets with salt, red pepper, coriander, and parsley. Add to the sous vide pouches, drizzle with olive oil and vacuum seal.

3. Submerge the pouches in the preheated water bath; allow the bagged fish to sous vide for 40 minutes.

4. Heat an oiled grill pan over high heat. Sear briefly for 2 to 3 minutes per side or until it forms a light golden crust.

5. Meanwhile, make the pesto by mixing macadamias, basil, mint, garlic, and lemon rind in your food processor. Pulse until coarsely chopped.

6. Now add the lemon juice and olive oil and continue mixing until fully incorporated; add a splash of water as needed. Serve macadamia pesto with warm fish fillets.

90. Dad's Classic Fried Shrimp

4 Servings

Ready in about
20 minutes

PER SERVING:
240 Calories; 11.9g Fat;
3.9g Carbs; 26.2g Protein;
0.0g Sugars

This recipe combines flavorful and perfectly cooked shrimp, dry white wine, and Mediterranean herbs into a decadent dinner that can be served with cornbread or pita bread.

Ingredients

- 2 tablespoons of olive oil
- 2 tablespoons of garlic, minced
- 1 teaspoon dried thyme
- 1 teaspoon dried rosemary
- 1/4 cup of dry white wine

- 1 pound of shrimp, peeled and deveined
- Sea salt, to taste
- 5-6 mixed peppercorns
- 1 tablespoon softened butter

Directions

1. Heat the oil in a saucepan that is preheated over a medium-high heat. Once hot, add the garlic and cook until just aromatic.

2. Now, stir in the thyme and rosemary and stir for 30 more seconds; add the wine, turn the heat to medium and cook until thoroughly warmed.

3. Add the pan mixture to the sous vide pouches; add the shrimp along with the salt and peppercorns.

4. Allow the bagged shrimp to sous vide in the preheated water bath at 130 degrees F for 15 minutes.

5. Melt the butter in a heavy-bottomed skillet and fry your shrimp, moving them around to ensure even cooking. Bon appétit!

91. SOLE FILLETS WITH FENNEL-APPLE SALAD

4 Servings

Ready in about
1 hour 5 minutes

PER SERVING:
353 Calories; 21.1g
Fat; 27.9g Carbs; 15.4g
Protein; 5.0g Sugars

There is nothing so delicious as a perfectly seared fish fillet – crispy crust and barely done meat in the middle. Once butter has melted, add the fish; don't forget to baste the fish with the butter frequently. These fillets pair perfectly with fresh fennel and apples.

Ingredients

- 4 sole fillets
- Salt and ground black pepper, to taste
- Zest of 1 medium-sized lemon
- 1 tablespoon fresh lemon juice
- 1 tablespoon champagne vinegar
- 1 tablespoon coconut sugar
- 2 sprigs of rosemary
- 2 whole cloves
- 1 teaspoon minced garlic
- 1 teaspoon cumin seeds

- 1 tablespoon fresh parsley leaves, roughly chopped
- 1 cup of water
- 2 tablespoons of butter, room temperature
- 1 fennel bulb, trimmed and thinly sliced
- 2 green-skinned apples, cored and diced
- 4 spring onions, sliced on the diagonal
- 3 tablespoons of Greek-style yogurt
- 3 tablespoons of mayonnaise
- 1 teaspoon Dijon mustard

Directions

1. Set the cooker to 130 degrees F.

2. Salt and pepper your fish. Then, mix the lemon zest, lemon juice, champagne vinegar, coconut sugar, rosemary, whole cloves, garlic, cumin, parsley and water in a large dish; add the fish fillets and let them marinate approximately 30 minutes.

3. Transfer the sole fillets to sous vide pouches. Submerge the pouches in the preheated water bath. Allow the fillets to sous vide for 30 to 35 minutes.

4. Remove the sole fillets from the pouches and pat them dry with a kitchen towel.

5. Melt the butter in a heavy skillet. After that quickly sear the fillets in hot butter; sear until crust forms.

6. Meanwhile, toss the remaining ingredients for the salad. Mound the salad onto a serving plate. Top with sole fillet and serve at once. Bon appétit!

92. Fish Tostadas with Coleslaw

4 Servings

Ready in about
40 minutes

PER SERVING:
526 Calories; 33.3g
Fat; 35.7g Carbs; 23.0g
Protein; 7.7g Sugars

Trout is cooked and wrapped in a warm corn tortilla. Yummy! Make for a casual meal with friends; serve with cocktails.

Ingredients

- 2 halibut steaks
- Kosher salt and ground black pepper, to taste
- 1 teaspoon cayenne pepper
- 1 oregano sprig
- 1 marjoram sprig
- 2 tablespoons of extra-virgin olive oil
- 1 tablespoon butter, room temperature
- 4 tostada shells

For the Coleslaw:

- 3 cups of cabbage, shredded
- 1/2 cup of carrots, shredded
- 1 yellow onion, thinly sliced
- 1/2 teaspoon fine sea salt
- 1 tablespoon brown sugar
- 2 tablespoons of Greek yogurt
- 1/2 cup of mayonnaise
- 1 teaspoon mustard
- A few drizzles of lemon juice

Directions

1. Set the cooker to 131 degrees F. Season your halibut with salt, black pepper, cayenne pepper, oregano, and marjoram. Drizzle with olive oil and transfer the steaks to sous vide bags.

2. When the water reaches the target temperature, lower the bagged halibut fish into the water; allow it to sous vide for 30 minutes.

3. When your halibut is ready, remove the bags from the water bath; pat the fish dry with pepper towels.

4. Then, preheat a sauté pan over a medium-high flame; add the butter. Once hot, sear the fish steaks until golden brown on the underside. Flip the halibut steaks and brown on the other side.

5. In the meantime, toss the cabbage with carrot and onion. Add the remaining ingredients for the coleslaw and stir until everything is well incorporated.

6. Afterwards, flake the halibut steaks into small pieces, discarding any remaining bones. Serve with tostadas and coleslaw.

93. Refreshing Scallop Salad

4 Servings

Ready in about
40 minutes
+ chilling time

PER SERVING:
199 Calories; 8.1g Fat;
11.2g Carbs; 20.5g
Protein; 3.6g Sugars

Sous vide your scallops and use them to arrange an outstanding salad. This lemon-vermouth vinaigrette is the perfect accompaniment to these perfectly cooked bay scallops. Quick and easy!

Ingredients

- 10 large-sized bay scallops
- 1 tablespoon fresh lemon juice
- 1 tablespoon oyster sauce
- 1 tablespoon dry vermouth
- 1 ½ tablespoons of olive oil
- 1 cup of cherry tomatoes, halved
- 1 cucumber, thinly sliced

- 4 spring onions, sliced lengthwise
- 1 large-sized carrot, trimmed and cut into matchsticks
- 1 teaspoon coarse salt
- 1/2 teaspoon dried dill weed
- 1/2 cup of Kalamata olives, pitted

Directions

1. Set your cooker to 140 degrees F.

2. Add the scallops to a sous vide bag. Allow them to sous vide for 35 minutes. After that, remove them from the bag and place in your refrigerator for 1 hour.

3. Meanwhile, make a vinaigrette by mixing the lemon juice, oyster sauce, dry vermouth, and olive oil.

4. Cut your scallops into halves. Divide among 4 individual plates and garnish with cherry tomato halves, cucumber, spring onions, and carrots.

5. Sprinkle with salt and dill; scatter Kalamata olives over everything and serve at once. Bon appétit!

94. THE PERFECT SEAFOOD ANTIPASTO

8 Servings

Ready in about
40 minutes

PER SERVING:
522 Calories; 35.4g Fat;
9.9g Carbs; 41.2g Protein;
0.0g Sugars

Serve up this antipasto of two kinds of fresh cheese, seafood, and vegetables that will satisfy your guests until the main course is ready.

Ingredients

- 1/2 pound of lobster
- 1/2 pound of shrimp, cleaned
- Sea salt and ground black pepper, to your liking
- 1 teaspoon hot paprika
- 2 tablespoons of olive oil
- 2 heads radicchio di Treviso, separated into leaves

- 1 pound of provolone cheese, cubed
- 1 pound of Bocconcini
- 1 cup of jarred roasted red and yellow peppers
- 1 cup of mixed olives
- 1/4 cup of Italian parsley, roughly chopped

Directions

1. Set your cooking machine to 126 degrees F. After that, place the lobster in the sous vide pouch; season with salt and black pepper to taste; add 1/2 teaspoon of hot paprika; drizzle with 1 tablespoon of olive oil.

2. Put the shrimp into another sous vide pouch; season with salt and black pepper and add the remaining 1/2 teaspoon of hot paprika; now, drizzle with the remaining 1 tablespoon of olive oil. Vacuum seal the pouches.

3. Submerge the pouches in the water bath. Sous vide for 35 minutes.

4. Line a serving platter with radicchio leaves. Arrange provolone cheese, bocconcini, roasted red and yellow peppers, seafood and olives on a platter in a decorative pattern.

5. Scatter fresh Italian parsley over everything. Bon appétit!

95. Drunken Mussels with Roasted Asparagus

6 Servings

Ready in about
1 hour

PER SERVING:
187 Calories; 2.8g Fat;
18.0g Carbs; 16.0g
Protein; 4.5g Sugars

Mussels are very delicate food and sous vide is one of the best techniques to cook them properly. Mussels are a great source of protein, selenium, Vitamin B12, Vitamin A and other valuable nutrients.

Ingredients

- 1 pound of asparagus, trimmed
- Salt and red pepper flakes, crushed
- 1/2 teaspoon garlic powder
- 1 teaspoon dried rosemary
- 1 ½ pounds of mussels, cleaned
- 1 carrot, trimmed and chopped

- 1 parsnip, trimmed and chopped
- 1 celery stalk, trimmed and chopped
- 1 leek, chopped
- 2 garlic cloves, minced
- 1 cup of sherry

Directions

1. Set the cooker to 183 degrees F. Add asparagus spears to sous vide pouches. Season with salt, red pepper, and garlic powder.

2. Cook your asparagus for 45 to 50 minutes. Sprinkle with rosemary and lightly grease with a nonstick cooking spray.

3. Then, roast the asparagus in the preheated oven at 450 degrees F about 10 minutes.

4. Turn the sous vide machine to 194 degrees F. Cook the mussels in the sous vide bags just for 2 minutes. Discard empty shells and scoop the flesh out of the opened shells.

5. Meanwhile, add the carrot, parsnip, celery, leek, and garlic to a large-sized saucepan. Cook over a moderate flame until the vegetables have softened.

6. Next, add the mussels and sherry. Let it simmer, covered, for about 3 minutes. Serve with grilled bread and lemon wedges. Bon appétit!

96. Elegant Tuna Steaks with Camembert and Apples

4 Servings

Ready in about
45 minutes

PER SERVING:
535 Calories; 27.5g
Fat; 17.0g Carbs; 54.4g
Protein; 11.9g Sugars

An elegant and simple dinner for any occasion. Tuna is an amazing food with supremely tender meat that literally melts in your mouth. In addition to being delicious, tuna fish is extremely healthy; it reduces blood pressure, improves our immune system, strengthens our bones, prevents cancer and much more.

Ingredients

- 4 tuna steaks
- 1/2 teaspoon ground black pepper, to taste
- 1/2 teaspoon cayenne pepper, or more to taste
- 1 teaspoon celery salt
- 1 ½ tablespoons of olive oil
- 1/2 cup of fresh chives, chopped

- 2 sprigs of rosemary, chopped
- 2 garlic cloves, chopped
- 1 ½ tablespoons of butter
- 1 teaspoon mixed peppercorns
- 2 Granny Smith apples, cored and diced
- 10 ounces of Camembert cheese
- 2 tablespoons of slivered almonds

Directions

1. Set your cooker to 127 degrees F. Now, season the tuna steaks with black pepper, cayenne pepper, and celery salt. Drizzle with olive oil.

2. Add the seasoned tuna steaks to the cooking pouches. Now, add fresh chives, rosemary, and garlic.

3. When the water reaches the target temperature, lower the bagged tuna into the water bath; allow it to sous vide for 30 to 35 minutes.

4. After, that, pat tuna steak dry with a dish cloth. Melt the butter in a sauté pan that is preheated over a medium-high flame.

5. Then, cook the peppercorns until they soften and pop, 4 to 5 minutes. Place the tuna steaks in the pan and cook to desired doneness.

6. Divide the steaks among four serving plates. Garnish with the apples and Camembert. Scatter almond slivers over everything and serve at once. Bon appétit!

97. SPICY AND DECADENT SEAFOOD SOUP

6 Servings

Ready in about
1 hour

PER SERVING:
164 Calories; 4.4g Fat;
10.8g Carbs; 18.5g
Protein; 5.8g Sugars

This is a slurp-worthy spicy soup that will fill your tummy for sure. Serve with enough homemade garlic bread or cheesy croutons for dunking.

Ingredients

- 1 ½ tablespoons of grapeseed oil
- 1 cup of yellow onions, minced
- 2 garlic cloves, thinly sliced
- 2 carrots, cleaned and chopped
- 1 parsnip, cleaned and chopped
- 1 turnip, cleaned and chopped
- 2 tablespoons of fish sauce
- 1 tablespoon soy sauce
- 1/3 cup of dry white wine

- 10 ounces of scallops, cleaned
- 10 ounces of tilapia, cut into strips
- 2 plum tomatoes, chopped
- 2 tablespoons of tomato ketchup
- 1/2 teaspoon hot chili sauce
- 1 teaspoon cumin powder
- 4 cups of water
- 1 tablespoon fresh cilantro, chopped

Directions

1. Set your cooker to 137 degrees F.

2. Preheat a heavy-bottomed skillet over a medium-high flame and add the oil. Once hot, sauté the onions, garlic, carrots, parsnip and turnip until they have softened. Transfer to the sous vide plastic bags.

3. Divide fish sauce, soy sauce, wine, scallops, tilapia, tomatoes, ketchup, hot chili sauce, and cumin powder among sous vide bags.

4. Allow them to sous vide for 50 to 55 minutes.

5. Now, transfer the cooked ingredients to a large-sized stock pot. Add 4 cups of water and bring to a rapid boil.

6. After that, reduce the heat to a simmer; let it simmer for an additional 5 minutes. Ladle into individual bowls, garnish with fresh cilantro, and serve immediately.

98. MELT-IN-YOUR-MOUTH MAHI-MAHI WITH PENNE

6 Servings

Ready in about
1 hour 10 minutes

PER SERVING:
285 Calories; 19.1g
Fat; 15.8g Carbs; 14.7g
Protein; 0.0g Sugars

Penne is one of the favorite pantry staples. Mahi-mahi is high in protein, vitamin B, iron and other valuable nutrients. Keep this recipe in your back pocket!

Ingredients

- 6 skinless mahi-mahi fillets, 3/4 inch thick
- 1/2 teaspoon ground black pepper, or more to taste
- 1 teaspoon fine sea salt
- 1 teaspoon Hungarian paprika
- 12 slices of grapefruit
- 3 tablespoons of olive oil
- 12 ounces of penne ziti
- 1 cup of mozzarella cheese, freshly grated
- 1/4 cup of packed fresh basil leaves, roughly chopped

Directions

1. Set your cooker to 141 degrees F.

2. Season bass fillets with ground black pepper, salt, and paprika. Place them in 6 separated cooking pouches; place 2 slices of grapefruit on each portion. Add 1/2 tablespoon of olive oil to each cooking pouch.

3. When the water bath reaches the target temperature, lower the bagged fish into the water and cook for 1 hour.

4. After that, quickly sear the fillets in hot butter until a nice crust forms. Cut into strips and reserve keeping warm.

5. Meanwhile, cook penne ziti al dente in a large pot of generously salted boiling water according to package directions; drain and divide among 6 individual plates.

6. Toss the penne with the reserved fish; top with mozzarella, garnish with fresh basil leaves and serve at once. Bon appétit!

99. STEELHEAD FILLET WITH CAPER SAUCE

4 Servings

Ready in about
20 minutes

PER SERVING:
225 Calories; 12.9g Fat;
27.3g Carbs; 2.8g Protein;
8.8g Sugars

Is there anything better than rich warm soup with fresh noodles? If you like a piquant flavor, drizzle each serving with the chili oil.

Ingredients

- Set your cooking machine to cook at 183 degrees F.

- Mix Brussels sprouts with olive oil, oyster sauce, brown sugar, sea salt flakes, ground black pepper, and red pepper flakes.

- Add the mixture to a vacuum bag. Seal the bag using a vacuum sealer on the dry setting. Remove as much air as possible.

- Place the bag in the water bath and set the timer for 35 minutes. You can serve it as a side dish or broil the Brussels sprouts until they are browned, 5 to 6 minutes.

- Garnish with fresh chopped cilantro. Bon appétit!

Directions

1. Set your cooking machine to cook at 183 degrees F.

2. Mix Brussels sprouts with olive oil, oyster sauce, brown sugar, sea salt flakes, ground black pepper, and red pepper flakes.

3. Add the mixture to a vacuum bag. Seal the bag using a vacuum sealer on the dry setting. Remove as much air as possible.

4. Place the bag in the water bath and set the timer for 35 minutes. You can serve it as a side dish or broil the Brussels sprouts until they are browned, 5 to 6 minutes.

5. Garnish with fresh chopped cilantro. Bon appétit!

1. Saucy Sweet Potatoes with Zucchini and Peppers

4 Servings

Ready in about
40 minutes

PER SERVING:
254 Calories; 18.4g Fat;
0.8g Carbs; 22.3g Protein;
0.0g Sugars

This classic fish recipe gets an "upgrade" with this citrusy and refreshing caper sauce. Serve with toasted focaccia bread and enjoy!

Ingredients

- 1 steelhead fillet, cut into 4 portions
- Sea salt flakes and cayenne pepper, to your liking
- 1 teaspoon shallot powder
- 1 teaspoon garlic powder
- 2 tablespoons of olive oil
- 2 sprigs of rosemary
- 1 sprig of oregano
- 1 tablespoon mixed peppercorns

For the sauce:
- 1 ½ tablespoons of softened butter
- 2 ½ tablespoons of fresh lemon juice
- 3/4 tablespoon drained capers, chopped
- 1 tablespoon fresh parsley, finely chopped

Directions

1. Season steelhead fillet with salt, cayenne pepper, shallot powder and garlic powder; massage the oil into the meat.

2. Divide the meat among sous vide pouches. Add rosemary, oregano, and mixed peppercorns.

3. Cook in the preheated water bath at 122 degrees F for 18 to 20 minutes. Pat fish dry with a dish cloth.

4. After that, preheat your oven to 450 degrees F. Line a rimmed baking sheet with parchment paper. Lay the prepared fish on the baking sheet. Grease with a nonstick cooking spray on all sides.

5. Roast in the oven for 15 to 17 minutes; check for doneness and adjust the seasonings.

6. In the meantime, thoroughly combine all the ingredients for the sauce; mix until well combined. Serve with warm fish. Bon appétit!

100. FALL SCALLOP AND SWEET POTATO SOUP

6 Servings

Ready in about
50 minutes

PER SERVING:
324 Calories; 17.5g
Fat; 30.2g Carbs; 13.6g
Protein; 5.9g Sugars

For this recipe, look for dry, pinkish scallops without additives. Serve with homemade cornbread, Kalamata olives and mellow Havarti cheese.

Ingredients

- 3/4 pounds of scallops, cleaned
- 1 teaspoon sea salt
- 1/2 teaspoon smoked cayenne pepper
- 1/2 teaspoon ground black pepper
- 3 tablespoons of extra-virgin olive oil
- 4 Vidalia onions, peeled and sliced
- 2 garlic cloves, peeled and minced
- 2 carrots, chopped

- 3/4 pounds of sweet potatoes
- 2 tablespoons of champagne vinegar
- 1 cup of coconut milk
- 1 ½ cups of vegetable broth
- 1 tablespoon dark soy sauce
- 1 tablespoon cornstarch, dissolved in 2 tablespoons of cold water

Directions

1. Set your cooker to 122 degrees F. Now, season the scallops with salt, smoked cayenne pepper, and black pepper. Transfer them to a sous vide bag and add 1 tablespoon of olive oil.

2. Allow them to sous vide for 35 minutes. Open the bag and remove your scallops.

3. In a soup pot, heat the remaining 2 tablespoons of olive oil. Once hot, cook Vidalia onions, garlic and carrots until just tender and aromatic.

4. Next, throw in the sweet potatoes and bring to a rolling boil. Reduce the heat to a simmer; add vinegar, milk, vegetables broth and soy sauce. Continue simmering for 8 to 12 minutes.

5. Afterwards, add the scallops and cornstarch slurry to the soup and stir for a few more minutes until everything is heated through. Serve warm in individual bowls. Bon appétit!

101. Easy Dilled Coho Salmon

6 Servings

Ready in about
50 minutes

PER SERVING:
298 Calories; 18.1g Fat;
2.7g Carbs; 34.6g Protein;
0.0g Sugars

Coho, also known as silver salmon, has numerous proven health benefits.
It's also called "brain food" because of the considerable amount of omega-3 fatty acids. Coho salmon is a great source of vitamin B12, Vitamin D, Selenium, Vitamin B3, Protein, and so on.

Ingredients

- 4 Coho salmon fillets
- 1 teaspoon smoked paprika
- 1/2 teaspoon seasoned salt
- 1/2 teaspoon pink peppercorns, freshly cracked

- 3 tablespoons of olive oil
- 1 teaspoon dill weed, fresh or frozen
- 1 lemon, cut into slices

Directions

1. Firstly, set the cooker to 140 degrees F. Season salmon fillets with smoked paprika, salt, and cracked peppercorns. Massage the fillets with 2 tablespoons of olive oil.

2. Transfer the salmon fillets to 4 sous vide bags. Lower the bags into the preheated water bath. Simmer for 40 minutes.

3. Place the remaining 1 tablespoon of olive oil in a nonstick skillet that is preheated over a moderate heat. Sprinkle each salmon fillet with chopped dill.

4. Sear for 2 to 3 minutes per side. Serve garnished with lemon slices and enjoy!

102. DIJON-STYLE MONKFISH FILLETS

6 Servings

Ready in about
55 minutes

PER SERVING:
272 Calories; 18.0g
Fat; 15.8g Carbs; 13.6g
Protein; 0.0g Sugars

If you've never made monkfish before, you'll find that it is actually very easy.
However, sous vide method makes everything simpler for you.

Ingredients

- 6 monkfish fillets
- Sea salt flakes and freshly ground black pepper, to your liking
- 1/2 teaspoon chipotle powder
- 2 tablespoons of tamari sauce
- 1 tablespoon oyster sauce

- 2 tablespoons of olive oil
- 1 tablespoon butter, room temperature
- 2 tablespoons of Dijon-style mustard
- 2 tablespoons of freshly chopped chives, for garnish

Directions

1. Set the cooker to 138 degrees F. Season the fish fillets with salt, black pepper, and chipotle powder.

2. Then, drizzle them with tamari sauce, oyster sauce and olive oil. Place each monkfish fillet in an individual pouch.

3. Submerge the pouches in the preheated water bath and simmer for 45 minutes.

4. Preheat a frying pan over a medium-high flame; melt the butter. Once hot, fry the monkfish along with Dijon-style mustard until golden brown on both sides.

5. Make sure to baste your fillets regularly. Garnish with fresh chives and serve on individual plates.

103. Oysters with Chipotle-Scallion Sauce

2 Servings

Ready in about
15 minutes

PER SERVING:
237 Calories; 5.3g Fat;
16.3g Carbs; 28.0g
Protein; 0.0g Sugars

This piquant sauce is a great accompaniment to sous vide oysters. Make the sauce at least 6 hours ahead of time to allow the flavors to blend.

Ingredients

- 30 oysters

For the Sauce:

- 1 Chipotle chili in Adobo, minced
- 1/2 cup of red wine vinegar
- 1 tablespoon ground black pepper

- 1/2 teaspoon red pepper flakes, crushed
- 4 scallions, chopped
- 1 teaspoon honey
- Sea salt flakes, to your liking

Directions

1. Set the cooker to 184 degrees F.

2. Coat a heat-safe gallon-size bag with a sheet of aluminum foil. Add your oysters and vacuum seal.

3. When the water reaches the target temperature, lower the bagged oysters; cook for 4 minutes.

4. Then, mix the remaining ingredients to prepare the sauce. Drizzle the sauce over warm oysters and serve with bread sticks. Bon appétit!

104. CREAMED LINGUINE WITH RAZOR CLAMS

4 Servings

Ready in about
15 minutes

PER SERVING:
492 Calories; 6.2g Fat;
77.9g Carbs; 29.0g
Protein; 8.3g Sugars

It's crazy easy to make this restaurant-style dinner! Sous vide razor clams and a sprinkle of Parmigiano-Reggiano give this linguine extra class!

Ingredients

- 1 pound of razor clams, cleaned and shells removed
- A splash of dry sherry
- 1 pound of linguine

- 1 ½ cups of pasta sauce
- 1/2 cup of Parmigiano-Reggiano, preferably freshly grated

Directions

1. Set your cooker to 212 degrees F.

2. Place razor clams in a sous vide cooking pouch and vacuum seal. Add a splash of dry sherry and lower the pouch into the preheated water bath.

3. Cook for 4 to 5 minutes. Remove the razor clams from the pouches.

4. Then, cook the linguine in a large pot of boiling salted water according to the manufacturer's directions. Drain and divide among four serving plates. Add pasta sauce and toss to combine.

5. Top with sous vide razor clams and Parmigiano-Reggiano. Bon appétit!

105. Chef's Secret Octopus Salad

8 Servings

Ready in about
5 hours

PER SERVING:
120 Calories; 5.9g Fat;
5.7g Carbs; 10.4g Protein;
2.5g Sugars

Is there anything better than rich warm soup with fresh noodles? If you like a piquant flavor, drizzle each serving with the chili oil.

Ingredients

- 2 pounds of octopus
- 2 tablespoons of dry white wine
- 2 whole cloves
- 1 sprig of rosemary, chopped
- 2 sprigs of thyme
- Sea salt flakes and ground black, to taste
- 3 tablespoons of extra-virgin olive oil

- 1 ½ tablespoons of fresh lemon juice
- 1 tablespoon fresh orange juice
- 1/3 cup of fresh parsley, chopped
- 2 garlic cloves, peeled and minced
- 1 cup of scallions, chopped
- 1 large-sized carrot, cut into matchsticks
- 1 ½ cups of Iceberg lettuce, torn into small pieces

Directions

1. Firstly, set your cooker to 170 degrees F. Pat your octopus dry with a dish cloth. Add to a large cooking pouch.

2. Then, throw in the wine, cloves, rosemary, thyme, salt, and ground black pepper. Allow the bagged octopus to cook for 5 hours.

3. Allow your octopus to cool and gently rub off any loose skin parts. Transfer to your refrigerator to cool completely.

4. Meanwhile, make the dressing by whisking the olive oil, freshly squeezed lemon juice, and orange juice.

5. Discard the head and cut the octopus into slices. Quickly sear them in the preheated saucepan to create a crispy outer layer, 1 to 2 minutes per side. Toss with remaining ingredients and transfer to a serving bowl.

6. Let stand for 30 to 45 minutes for flavors to develop. Bon appétit!

VEGAN

106

110

114

117

104

106. Brussels Sprouts with Hummus Sauce

4 Servings

Ready in about
45 minutes

PER SERVING:
123 Calories; 7.4g Fat;
13.2g Carbs; 4.5g Protein;
4.1g Sugars

Looking for a simple vegan recipe to delight your guests? This recipe is both delicious and sophisticated. You can substitute agave nectar for brown sugar and coconut oil for peanut oil.

Ingredients

- 1 pound of Brussels sprouts
- 1 sprig of oregano
- 1 sprig of rosemary
- 1 sprig of thyme
- 2 tablespoons of peanut oil
- 1/2 cup of basic hummus, preferably homemade
- 1 teaspoon Hungarian paprika

- 1 ½ tablespoons of fresh lime juice
- 1 tablespoon fresh orange juice
- 1 teaspoon onion powder
- 1 teaspoon garlic powder
- 1 teaspoon cumin powder
- 1 teaspoon brown sugar
- 1/2 cup of fresh chopped chives

Directions

1. Set your cooker to 158 degrees F. Trim the bottom of each of the Brussels sprouts; cut each in half top to bottom.

2. Place Brussels sprouts along with oregano, rosemary, thyme and peanut oil in a heat-safe gallon-size bag; vacuum seal.

3. Allow them to sous vide for 40 minutes.

4. Meanwhile, make the sauce by mixing the hummus with paprika, lime juice, orange juice, onion powder, garlic powder, cumin powder, and brown sugar. Mix to combine well.

5. Garnish with chopped chives and serve with cooked Brussels sprouts. Bon appétit!

107. Skinny Cremini Mushrooms with Mustard Gravy

4 Servings

Ready in about
1 hour 15 minutes

PER SERVING:
137 Calories; 7.3g Fat;
12.4g Carbs; 6.1g Protein;
2.1g Sugars

Cremini mushrooms are high in Vitamin D, potassium, B Vitamins, fiber, antioxidants, and so forth. A strong flavor of whole-grain mustard allows the mild and hearty flavors of the mushrooms to shine.

Ingredients

- 1 pound of Cremini mushrooms
- 2 garlic cloves, peeled and pressed
- 2 tablespoons of grapeseed oil
- 1 tablespoon soy sauce
- 1 tablespoon dry white wine
- 1 sprig of oregano, chopped
- 1 sprig of rosemary, chopped
- 2 whole cloves

- 1 teaspoon grated fresh ginger
- 1 teaspoon sea salt flakes
- 1/4 teaspoon ground black pepper, or more to taste
- 3/4 cup of vegetable stock
- 2 tablespoons of cornstarch
- 2 ½ tablespoons of nutritional yeast
- 1 tablespoon whole-grain mustard

Directions

1. Set your cooker to 183 degrees F.

2. Add your mushrooms to a large-sized cooking pouch. Throw in the garlic, oil, soy sauce, wine, oregano, rosemary, cloves, ginger, salt, and black pepper.

3. Now, shake to distribute evenly and vacuum seal. Allow the bagged mushrooms to sous vide for 1 hour 10 minutes.

4. Preheat your saucepan over a moderate flame. Pour in the stock, bringing to a gentle simmer; now, throw in cooked mushrooms and continue simmering for a further 5 minutes.

5. After that, slowly add the cornstarch, whisking constantly to prevent lumps. Take your pan off the heat and stir in nutritional yeast and mustard. Serve immediately.

108. GARLICKY CAULIFLOWER WITH VIDALIA ONIONS

4 Servings

Ready in about
1 hour 45 minutes

PER SERVING:
100 Calories; 6.9g Fat;
8.8g Carbs; 2.4g Protein;
3.3g Sugars

Are you ready for a light and nutritious vegan dinner? Cauliflower is a powerhouse of vitamins, minerals, and fiber. Serve with tofu cheese on the side.

Ingredients

- 1 pound of cauliflower florets
- 1/2 Vidalia onions, peeled
- 2 tablespoons of grapeseed oil
- 1 small-sized garlic head, peeled and chopped

- Sea salt flakes and ground black pepper, to taste
- 1/4 teaspoon red pepper flakes, crushed
- 1 teaspoon agave nectar
- 2 tablespoons of fresh cilantro leaves

Directions

1. Set your cooker to 183 degrees F. Place the cauliflower florets in a single layer in a sous vide bag; seal the bag.

2. In another sous vide bag, place the Vidalia onions; vacuum seal. Lower the bags into the water bath and set the timer for 1 hour 30 minutes. Remove the vegetables from the bags and pat them dry. Reserve the cooked Vidalia onions.

3. Toss the cauliflower with oil, garlic, salt, black pepper, red pepper, and agave nectar.

4. Then, preheat your oven to 425 degrees F. Spread the cauliflower florets evenly on baking sheet and roast until golden, about 15 minutes.

5. Adjust the seasonings and garnish with fresh cilantro. Serve with reserved Vidalia onions. Bon appétit!

109. THANKSGIVING SQUASH WITH RED KIDNEY BEANS

4 Servings

Ready in about
1 hour

PER SERVING:
425 Calories; 8.2g Fat;
70.1g Carbs; 22.1g
Protein; 3.1g Sugars

Get inspired by squash and kidney beans this holiday season. If you like your veggies spicy, add a few dashes of Tabasco.

Ingredients

- 1 winter squash, peeled and sliced
- 2 tablespoons of olive oil
- 3 garlic cloves, pressed
- 1 can of red kidney beans
- Salt and ground black pepper, to your liking

- 1 teaspoon hot paprika
- 1/4 teaspoon cumin powder
- 1/2 teaspoon ground coriander
- 1 can of petite diced tomatoes

Directions

1. Set your cooker to 175 degrees F. Place your squash in a zip-top bag.

2. Allow the bagged squash to sous vide for 50 minutes.

3. Heat olive oil in a pan over a moderate flame. Now, sauté the garlic until just browned and aromatic.

4. Stir in the remaining ingredients along with the reserved squash. Cook for 5 to 8 minutes or until the beans are fairly soft. Serve warm.

110. Mom's Spicy and Saucy Tofu

4 Servings

Ready in about
1 hour 15 minutes

PER SERVING:
134 Calories; 4.0g Fat;
16.7g Carbs; 9.0g Protein;
3.5g Sugars

Ketjap manis is an Indonesian version of soy sauce. Keep in mind that it contains palm sugar and it is well known as a sweet soy sauce. Still, it has a piquant and rich taste as well as syrupy texture.

Ingredients

- 1 ½ cups of vegetable broth
- 1 teaspoon hot sauce
- 4 garlic cloves, minced
- 1 tablespoon of Ketjap manis
- 1 tablespoon molasses

- 1 tablespoon apple cider vinegar
- 1/2 teaspoon ground clove
- 1/2 teaspoon onion powder
- 1/2 pounds of extra-firm tofu, cut into cubes

Directions

1. Set your cooker to 183 degrees F.

2. In a mixing dish, thoroughly combine the broth, hot sauce, garlic, Ketjap manis, molasses, vinegar, clove, and onion powder; mix until everything is well incorporated.

3. Add the prepared sauce to a cooking pouch; throw in tofu cubes and vacuum seal.

4. Lower the bag into the preheated water bath and cook for 1 hour 15 minutes.

5. Serve immediately with crusty bread and with lots of fresh salad. Bon appétit!

111. Famous Beet and Arugula Salad

4 Servings

Ready in about
55 minutes
+ chilling time

PER SERVING:
170 Calories; 14.0g Fat;
11.2g Carbs; 2.5g Protein;
7.5g Sugars

If you don't prefer citrus fruit, just skip it in this recipe, without sacrificing a flavor. This is entirely a matter of personal preference!

Ingredients

- 2 beetroots, peeled and cut into thick slices
- 1/2 teaspoon table salt
- 1/4 cup of olive oil
- 1 tablespoon cider vinegar
- 1 teaspoon lemon juice, freshly squeezed
- 1 teaspoon orange juice, freshly squeezed
- 1 purple onion, peeled and thinly sliced

- 2 cups of fresh arugula
- 1/2 teaspoon seasoned salt, or more to your liking
- 1/2 teaspoon ground black pepper, or more to your liking
- 1 teaspoon cumin seeds
- 1 tablespoon toasted pumpkin seeds

Directions

1. Set your cooking machine to 183 degrees F. Sprinkle the slices of beets with salt.

2. Add the beets to a cooking pouch and vacuum seal. Allow the bagged beets to sous vide for 55 minutes.

3. Allow the cooked beets to cool completely in your refrigerator. Then, toss them with the olive oil, cider vinegar, lemon juice, orange juice, onion, and arugula.

4. Then, sprinkle with the seasoned salt, along with the pepper and cumin seeds. Toss to combine well, garnish with pumpkin seeds and serve. Bon appétit!

112. COLORFUL VEGGIE DELIGHT

4 Servings

Ready in about
1 hour 40 minutes

PER SERVING:
357 Calories; 29.0g Fat;
25.0g Carbs; 4.7g Protein;
13.9g Sugars

With several layers of flavor, this colorful and rich vegan meal always turns out perfect by using sous vide cooker. Serve with homemade cornbread.

Ingredients

- 2 Roma tomatoes, sliced
- 2 zucchinis, sliced
- 3 sweet peppers, deveined and sliced
- 1 eggplant, sliced
- 1 leek, cut into thick slices
- 1 teaspoon sea salt flakes, or more to taste
- 1 teaspoon smoked cayenne pepper
- 1/2 teaspoon green peppercorns, freshly cracked

- 1 small-sized garlic head, pressed
- 1/2 cup of peanut oil
- 2 tablespoons of tomato ketchup
- 1/4 teaspoon hot sauce
- 1 heaping tablespoon Italian parsley
- 1 heaping tablespoon toasted sesame seeds

Directions

1. Set your cooker to 183 degrees F. Place each type of vegetable in its own sous vide bag. Season with salt, cayenne pepper, and cracked green peppercorns.

2. Divide the garlic among the sous vide bags. Divide the oil among bags and vacuum seal. When the water reaches the target temperature, lower the bags into the water bath; make sure that your bags are fully submerged

3. Allow the bagged vegetables to sous vide for 35 minutes. Now, remove the bag with the tomatoes; reserve. Set the timer for another 35 more minutes.

4. Now, remove the bags with the zucchini and sweet peppers. Reserve. Set the timer for an additional 30 minutes to cook the bagged eggplant and leeks.

5. Afterwards, chop your vegetables and toss them with ketchup and hot sauce. Serve garnished with parsley and sesame seeds. Bon appétit!

113. Decadent Eggplant, Peanut and Shallot Soup

6 Servings

Ready in about
1 hour 20 minutes

PER SERVING:
251 Calories; 15.7g Fat;
20.9g Carbs; 8.5g Protein;
6.3g Sugars

You know those soup recipes that take a full day to cook? This rich eggplant soup recipe isn't one of them. Serve at room temperature or cold with the garlic croutons on the side.

Ingredients

- 2 eggplants
- 4 tablespoons of grapeseed oil
- 4 garlic cloves, minced
- 1 ½ cups of shallots, peeled and chopped
- 1/4 teaspoon black peppercorns, freshly cracked
- 1/4 teaspoon green peppercorns, freshly cracked

- 1 teaspoon kosher salt
- 4 cups of vegetable broth
- 1 tablespoon freshly squeezed lime juice
- 1 tablespoon balsamic vinegar
- 1/4 cup of chunky natural peanut butter
- 1 tablespoon fresh cilantro, roughly chopped

Directions

1. Set your device to 183 degrees F. Now, rinse the eggplant and cut it into thick slices.

2. Transfer the eggplant to the sous vide pouch. Allow the bagged eggplant to sous vide for 1 hour. Remove the bag from the water bath and reserve.

3. Then, heat the oil in a large soup pot; once hot, sauté the garlic and shallots until just tender and aromatic.

4. Add the peppercorns, salt, and reserved eggplant; allow them to cook for 1 to 2 minutes longer. Now, add the vegetable broth and let it simmer for 8 to 12 minutes.

5. Afterwards, take the pot off the heat; add fresh lime juice, vinegar and peanut butter. Puree with an immersion hand blender until well mixed. Taste and adjust the seasonings.

6. Ladle into individual bowls, garnish with fresh cilantro, and serve with a few drizzles of olive oil. Bon appétit!

114. Velvety Carrot Soup with Cashew Sour Cream

4 Servings

Ready in about
2 hours 15 minutes

PER SERVING:
170 Calories; 9.7g Fat;
19.2g Carbs; 3.2g Protein;
5.7g Sugars

What we love most about using sous vide to cook vegetables is that we can leave the cooker unattended. Finished with amazingly creamy cashew sour cream, this is a knockout entrée for any occasion!

Ingredients

- 3/4 pounds of carrots, cut into thick slices
- 1 turnip, diced
- 1 tablespoon coconut oil
- 1 cup of shallots, diced
- 2 vegetable bouillon cubes
- 3/4 teaspoon turmeric powder

- 1/4 teaspoon garlic powder
- 1/4 teaspoon cumin powder
- 1/2 teaspoon mixed peppercorns, freshly cracked
- 3 cups of water
- 1/2 cup of cashew sour cream
- Fresh tarragon leaves, for garnish

Directions

1. Set your cooker to 183 degrees F.

2. Place your carrots and turnip in sous vide pouches; add a splash of water and vacuum seal. Allow them to sous vide for 2 hours.

3. In a stock pot, warm the oil and swirl to coat the entire bottom. Once hot, sauté your shallots until translucent.

4. After that, add the bouillon cubes along with turmeric powder, garlic powder, cumin powder, peppercorns, and water. Throw in the cooked carrot and turnip.

5. Cook for 15 minutes or until everything is heated through. Allow your soup to cool slightly and fold in cashew sour cream. Now, purée the soup with an immersion hand blender.

6. Ladle into individual bowls; serve garnished with fresh tarragon leaves. Bon appétit!

115. Green Bean and Fennel Salad with Pecans

4 Servings

Ready in about
1 hour
+ chilling time

PER SERVING:
174 Calories; 14.3g Fat;
11.8g Carbs; 3.1g Protein;
1.3g Sugars

It doesn't take a lot of effort to turn an ordinary vegan salad into an outstanding, crave-worthy light meal. Make your salad more nutritious by adding 1 to 2 heaping tablespoons of nutritional yeast or tofu cubes. Be inspired!

Ingredients

- 3/4 pounds of green beans
- 1/2 pounds of fennel bulbs
- 4 garlic cloves, pressed
- 1 tablespoon raspberry vinaigrette

- 1/4 cup of extra-virgin olive oil
- Kosher salt and crushed red pepper flakes, to taste
- 2 tablespoons of pecans, roughly chopped

Directions

1. Set your cooker to 183 degrees F.

2. Add green beans to a cooking pouch; in another pouch, place the fennel bulbs. Vacuum seal and allow the vegetables to sous vide for 1 hour.

3. Remove the vegetables from the pouches. Allow them to cool completely in your refrigerator.

4. Toss with the other items and serve at once!

116. Fresh Summer Salad with Garlic Confit

4 Servings

Ready in about
1 hour 20 minutes

PER SERVING:
174 Calories; 14.3g Fat;
11.8g Carbs; 3.1g Protein;
1.3g Sugars

This recipe may sound a little snobbish, but garlic confit is a regular garlic cooked in pure olive oil. Cook's note: Always bring garlic confit to room temperature before using.

Ingredients

- 1 garlic head, peeled and separated into cloves
- 1 bay leaf
- 1 chile de arbol, dried
- 2 sprigs of thyme
- 2 sprigs of rosemary
- 1/4 cup of olive oil
- 1 ½ teaspoons of salt

For the Salad:

- 2 plum tomatoes, diced
- 1 cucumber, thinly sliced
- 1 avocado, pitted and sliced
- 2 sweet peppers
- 1 ½ tablespoons of alfalfa sprouts
- Toasted bread cubes, for garnish

Directions

1. Set your cooker to 192 degrees F.

2. Throw the garlic cloves, bay leaf, chile de árbol, thyme, rosemary, and olive oil into a sous vide pouch.

3. Once hot, submerge the bagged garlic in the water; cook for 1 hour 20 minutes. Allow it to chill slightly. After that, pat the garlic cloves dry with a dish cloth.

4. Next, transfer the garlic, herbs and chiles to a canning jar; add the salt. Fill your jar with cooking oil and seal. Keep covered in oil for up to 4 months in your refrigerator.

5. In a salad bowl, toss together the tomato, cucumber, avocado, sweet peppers, and alfalfa sprouts. Slice garlic cloves in half and toss them into your salad.

6. Scatter bread cubes over the salad and serve at once. Bon appétit!

117. THE BEST VEGAN PILAF EVER

4 Servings

Ready in about
1 hour 15 minutes

PER SERVING:
320 Calories; 4.2g Fat;
63.9g Carbs; 5.8g Protein;
3.0g Sugars

Sous vide allows you to cook your veggies at the desired temperature so there is less risk of under- or overcooking them. Hence it is not surprising that sous vide method has caught fire around the world!

Ingredients

- 2 carrots, trimmed and chopped
- 1 small-sized broccoli head, broken into florets
- 1 white onion, chopped
- 3 garlic cloves, smashed
- 1 teaspoon dried marjoram
- 1 teaspoon dried rosemary
- 1 tablespoon olive oil

- 1 ½ cups of Arborio rice
- 3 ½ cups of water
- 1/4 teaspoon cumin powder
- 1/2 teaspoon paprika
- 2 vegetable bouillon cubes
- Kosher salt and ground black pepper, to taste

Directions

1. Set the cooker to 183 degrees F. Throw each type of vegetable into a separate bag. Divide the garlic, marjoram, rosemary and olive oil between the bags.

2. Set the timer for 30 minutes. Remove the bagged broccoli and onion.

3. Now, add the rice along with the water, cumin powder, paprika, and vegetable bouillon cubes to the separated cooking pouch. Set the timer for another 45 minutes.

4. Remove your rice from the pouch, taste for doneness and combine with the prepared vegetables. Salt and pepper to taste. Serve immediately.

118. SQUASH AND PEAR SOUP WITH VEGAN CRÈME FRAICHE

4 Servings

Ready in about
1 hour

PER SERVING:
367 Calories; 28.5g Fat;
27.2g Carbs; 4.1g Protein;
17.5g Sugars

It's no shocker that sous vide conquered the world! Sous vide technique makes eating all vegetables as delicious as anything else. If you want to go full veg, this recipe yields a quick and flavorful treat.

Ingredients

- 1 summer squash, peeled and diced
- 2 firm ripe Bartlett pears, peeled, cored, and diced
- 1 Vidalia onion, peeled and diced
- 2 sprigs of oregano
- Sea salt and ground white pepper, to your liking
- 1 teaspoon fresh ginger root, minced
- 1/2 teaspoon ground allspice

- 1/2 teaspoon coriander, minced
- 1 ½ cups of roasted vegetable broth

For the Vegan Crème fraiche:
- 1/2 cup of soymilk
- 1 teaspoon fresh lime juice
- 1/2 cup of sesame oil
- 1 tablespoon agave nectar

Directions

1. Set your cooker to 183 degrees F.

2. Add the squash, pears, onion, oregano, salt, and white pepper to a sous vide pouch; vacuum seal. Allow the mixture to sous vide for 55 minutes.

3. In the meantime, make the vegan cream by mixing soymilk and lime juice in your blender; reserve. Pulse sesame oil with agave nectar until well blended; slowly and gradually pour the oil mixture into the soymilk mixture. Mix until everything has thickened.

4. Then, transfer your vegetables from the sous vide pouch to the pot. Stir in minced ginger, allspice, coriander, broth, and prepared cream.

5. Mix with an immersion hand blender until uniform and very creamy. Serve at room temperature or chilled. Enjoy!

119. MEDITERRANEAN VEGETABLE SKILLET

4 Servings

Ready in about
1 hour 30 minutes

PER SERVING:
360 Calories; 13.5g
Fat; 51.2g Carbs; 12.3g
Protein; 11.1g Sugars

If you take a closer look at the nutritional content of this meal, you will be amazed. This skillet is full of valuable nutrients such as proteins, vitamin A, dietary fiber, manganese, and so on.

Ingredients

- 1/2 pound of Yukon gold potatoes, cubed
- 2 carrots, sliced
- 1 parsnip, sliced
- 1 jalapeño pepper, deveined and minced
- Sea salt and ground black pepper, to your liking
- 1 tablespoon peanut oil
- 1 sprig of thyme
- 2 sprigs of rosemary

- 1 sprig of oregano
- 1 ½ tablespoons of olive oil
- 1 purple onion, chopped
- 4 garlic cloves, minced
- 1 tablespoon fresh basil, finely chopped
- 1 tablespoon fresh sage, finely chopped
- 1 tomato, chopped
- 1 can garbanzo beans
- 2 tablespoons of slivered almonds

Directions

1. Set your cooker to 185 degrees F. Add each type of vegetable to a separate sous vide bag. Divide the minced jalapeño pepper, salt, black pepper, peanut oil, thyme, rosemary and oregano among your bags.

2. Now, arrange the bags on a rack. Once hot, lower the bags into the preheated water bath. Set the timer for 1 hour 30 minutes.

3. Warm the olive oil in a heavy skillet that is preheated over a moderate flame. Sauté the onion and garlic until just tender and aromatic.

4. Stir in fresh basil and sage; add chopped tomato and continue cooking until heated through.

5. Throw in garbanzo beans and cooked vegetables. Remove from the heat and adjust the seasonings. Serve garnished with almond slivers. Bon appétit!

120. SHERRIED BUTTERNUT SQUASH BISQUE WITH CHERVIL

6 Servings

Ready in about
1 hour 20 minutes

PER SERVING:
219 Calories; 14.9g Fat;
19.9g Carbs; 4.5g Protein;
5.7g Sugars

This fall recipe showcases the season's best flavors! In this recipe, you can substitute acorn squash for butternut squash. Sweet yellow-fleshed squash is one of the healthiest foods in the world! It improves your immune system, fights cancer, protects your heart, controls PMS symptoms, and so forth.

Ingredients

- 1 ½ pounds of butternut squash, peeled and diced
- 1 ¼ cups of almond milk
- 1 tablespoon ground ginger
- 1 teaspoon maple syrup
- 1 teaspoon fennel seeds
- 1 tablespoon sesame oil

- 1 small yellow onion, peeled and chopped
- 1 garlic clove, chopped
- 2 tablespoons of dry sherry
- 2 cups of vegetable broth
- 1 tablespoon fresh lemon juice
- 1/4 cup of fresh chervil, chopped

Directions

1. Set your device to 183 degrees F. Add the squash to sous vide bags.

2. Then, thoroughly combine the almond milk, ginger, maple syrup, and fennel seeds. Add this mixture to the sous vide bags with squash.

3. When the water bath reaches the desired temperature, lower the bagged squash into the water. Allow to sous vide for 1 hour.

4. Heat the sesame oil in a stock pot. Then, sauté the onions until translucent. Now, stir in the garlic and cook until just browned. Add dry sherry and stir to deglaze the pot.

5. Pour in the vegetable broth and bring to a rolling boil. After that, reduce the heat to a simmer. Let your soup simmer for 12 to 15 minutes.

6. Add lemon juice and puree in your blender, working in batches. Serve at room temperature garnished with fresh chervil. Bon appétit!

SNACKS & APPETIZERS

122

125

130

135

139

121. PARTY MINTY GRILLED MEATBALLS WITH SAUCE

8 Servings

Ready in about
1 hour 30 minutes

PER SERVING:
150 Calories; 4.5g Fat;
10.6g Carbs; 15.9g
Protein; 6.1g Sugars

Discover new ways to prepare your party menu. Grilled meatballs are heavenly delicious and super-versatile party snack. This time, they are served with zingy, sticky sauce.

Ingredients

For the Meatballs:

- 1/2 pound of ground pork
- 1/2 pound of ground turkey
- 1/3 cup crushed saltines
- 2 tablespoons of milk
- 2 garlic cloves, minced
- 1 tablespoon minced fresh mint
- 1/2 teaspoon ground cumin

For the Sauce:

- 1/3 cup of water
- 1/3 cup of dark brown sugar
- 1/2 cup of Ketjap manis
- 1/3 cup of vermouth
- 1 teaspoon fresh ginger, grated
- Salt and ground black pepper, to taste

Directions

1. Set your cooker to 138 degrees F.

2. Combine all ingredients for the meatballs until everything is well incorporated. You may need more or less crushed saltines to knead the mixture well.

3. Form the mixture into 20 meatballs. Place your meatballs in a single layer in sous vide bags.

4. Cook in the preheated water bath for 1 hour 20 minutes. Remove the bags from the bath.

5. After that, grill your meatballs over a moderate heat, about 2 minutes per side.

6. Meanwhile, prepare the sauce. In a deep pan, bring the water and sugar to a rolling boil, whisking until sugar completely dissolves.

7. Turn the heat to a medium-low; add the remaining ingredients for the sauce. Let it simmer, until thickened and reduced by half, approximately 35 minutes.

8. Arrange the meatballs on a serving platter; add cocktail sticks. Serve the sauce on the side. Bon appétit!

122. Crispy Tenga with Blood Orange Gastrique

8 Servings

Ready in about
22 hours
+ marinating time

PER SERVING:
219 Calories; 11.6g Fat;
21.4g Carbs; 9.0g Protein;
17.5g Sugars

Pig's ears are cooked sous vide and then deep-fried. The end result is bites that are crispy and delicious. A tart-sweet gastrique perfectly pairs with them.

Ingredients

- 4 pig's ears, cleaned
- Sea salt and ground black pepper, to your liking
- 4 garlic cloves, minced
- 1 sprig of thyme, chopped
- 1 sprig of rosemary, chopped
- 6 tablespoons of vegetable oil

For Blood Orange Gastrique:
- 4 tablespoons of brown sugar
- 2 tablespoons of champagne vinegar
- 6 blood oranges, freshly squeezed
- 1 ¾ cups of chicken broth

Directions

1. Season the pig's ears with salt and ground black pepper on all sides.

2. Add each ear to a separate bag; divide the garlic, thyme and rosemary among the bags. Then, refrigerate them, sealed, for 2 days.

3. Set your cooker to 183 degrees F.

4. After that, rinse the pig's ears under running water; pat them dry with a kitchen towel. Put each of them into a sous vide bag; add 1 ½ tablespoons of vegetable oil to each bag.

5. Lower the bags into the preheated water bath; allow the bagged ears to sous vide for 22 hours.

6. Then, deep-fry the pig's ears, working in batches; drain them on paper towels and season to taste. Cut into slices and arrange on a serving platter.

7. To make the gastrique, melt the sugar in a pan over a moderate heat. Cook until golden, 4 to 6 minutes. Slowly add champagne vinegar, whisking constantly for 1 to 2 minutes.

8. Pour in orange juice and cook for an additional 5 minutes; pour in chicken broth; let it boil until gastrique has thickened. Serve with well-seasoned pig ear strips.

123. Honey-Glazed Carrot Matchsticks

8 Servings

Ready in about
1 hour 30 minutes

PER SERVING:
99 Calories; 5.8g Fat;
12.2g Carbs; 0.8g Protein;
7.5g Sugars

Fresh carrots, seasoning and honey are magically transformed into a flavorsome, sophisticated snack that is healthy as well! Fresh cilantro and nutritional yeast work well for garnish.

Ingredients

- 1 ¼ pounds of carrots, peeled and cut into matchsticks
- Sea salt and red pepper flakes, to taste
- 2 ½ tablespoons of olive oil
- 1/2 teaspoon dill weed, fresh or dried
- 1 tablespoon honey

Directions

1. Set your cooker to 183 degrees F. Place carrots in the sous vide cooking pouches; then, divide salt, red pepper flakes, and olive oil among the pouches.

2. Allow the bagged carrots to sous vide for 1 hour 15 minutes. Throw the contents of the bags into the preheated skillet; add fresh or dried dill and stir for 2 to 3 minutes.

3. Stir in the honey and cook until heated through. Bon appétit!

124. CRISPY MEDITERRANEAN-STYLE CHIPS

6 Servings

Ready in about
1 hour 40 minutes

PER SERVING:
144 Calories; 4.7g Fat;
23.8g Carbs; 2.5g Protein;
1.7g Sugars

Never underestimate the importance of good crispy chips at a dinner party. Inspired by this classic, you can come up with the snack that is just scrumptious! To make it more Mediterranean, serve with Kalamata olives.

Ingredients

*   2 pounds of potatoes, peeled and diced
*   2 tablespoons of olive oil
*   Sea salt flakes, to your liking
*   2 sprigs of rosemary
*   2 sprigs of oregano
*   1 teaspoon mixed peppercorns
*   1 teaspoon kosher salt, plus more for serving

Directions

1. Set your cooking machine to 185 degrees F. Divide the potatoes among two sous vide bags. Add 1 tablespoon of olive oil, 1 rosemary sprig, an oregano sprig and a few peppercorns to each bag; vacuum seal.

2. When the water bath reaches the desired temperature, lower the bags into the water; cook for 1 hour 30 minutes.

3. Remove the potatoes from the bags and pat them dry with a dish cloth.

4. Heat oil in a deep-fryer to 375 degrees F. Fry your potatoes until golden, approximately 6 minutes. Finally, taste for doneness, adjust the seasonings, and serve immediately with your favorite tomato ketchup.

125. Asiago-Kale Dip with Crudités

10 Servings

Ready in about
40 minutes

PER SERVING:
114 Calories; 9.7g Fat;
3.8g Carbs; 3.5g Protein;
0.7g Sugars

Crudités and dips! Sounds like a great party! Use fresh kale leaves to create this rich dip as well as Asiago that tastes amazing, lending satisfying deliciousness to your dip.

Ingredients

- 2 cups kale leaves, ribs removed
- 1 teaspoon kosher salt
- 1/2 teaspoon red pepper flakes, crushed
- 2 tablespoons of olive oil
- 1/3 cup of mayonnaise

- 2 tablespoons of sour cream
- Salt and ground black pepper, to taste
- 1 teaspoon garlic powder
- 1/2 teaspoon mustard powder
- 1 cup of Asiago cheese, shredded

Directions

1. Set your cooker to 190 degrees F.

2. Toss the kale leaves with salt, red pepper, and olive oil. Transfer to a large-sized sous vide bag and cook for 8 minutes.

3. Transfer to a mixing bowl. Add mayonnaise, sour cream, salt, black pepper, garlic powder, and mustard powder. Fold in 1/2 cup of shredded Asiago cheese.

4. Stir until everything is well incorporated. Scrape into a lightly oiled casserole dish; top with remaining 1/2 cup of Asiago cheese.

5. Bake in the preheated oven at 420 degrees F for 30 minutes. Serve with crudités and enjoy!

126. Cheesy Corn on the Cob with Chives

6 Servings

Ready in about
35 minutes

PER SERVING:
185 Calories; 7.6g Fat;
29.5g Carbs; 5.1g Protein;
5.3g Sugars

Corn on the cob is definitely one of the best options to make your snack time a delicious pleasure. In this recipe, you can substitute freshly grated Parmigiano-Reggiano for Fontina with the same results.

Ingredients

- 6 ears of corn, still in the husk, both ends trimmed
- 1 teaspoon salt
- 1/4 teaspoon red pepper, crushed
- 1/4 teaspoon garlic powder

- 1/2 teaspoon shallot powder
- 3 tablespoons of butter, softened
- Freshly chopped chives, for garnish
- Grated Fontina cheese, for garnish

Directions

1. Set your cooker to 183 degrees F. Divide the corn among two sous vide pouches. Season with salt, red pepper, garlic powder, and shallot powder.

2. Divide the butter among your pouches and vacuum seal. Allow the bagged corn to sous vide for 35 minutes.

3. Afterwards, discard the husks, and serve with fresh chives and grated Fontina cheese. Bon appétit!

127. EASY BACON WRAPPED PINEAPPLE APPETIZER

12 Servings

Ready in about
8 hours 10 minutes

PER SERVING:
205 Calories; 15.8g Fat;
0.5g Carbs; 14.0g Protein;
0.0g Sugars

Use these fun bites as the perfect party starter! You can substitute banana chunks
for the pineapple cubes.

Ingredients

- 12 slices of bacon
- 24 pineapple cubes

- Cocktail sticks

Directions

1. Set your cooker to 145 degrees F. Place the bacon slices in the sous vide bags; vacuum seal.

2. Cook for 8 hours. Cut each bacon slice into halves lengthwise. Wrap each pineapple cube with a bacon slice.

3. Broil the bacon-wrapped pineapple, flipping halfway, until crisp and just browned, 7 to 9 minutes. Serve on a serving platter with cocktail sticks. Bon appétit!

128. TWICE-COOKED FRENCH FRIES WITH GUACAMOLE

8 Servings

Ready in about
50 minutes

PER SERVING:
158 Calories; 6.9g Fat;
22.3g Carbs; 2.4g Protein;
1.6g Sugars

These French fries are crispy on the outside and perfectly cooked in the center.
The mild flavor of potatoes balances out the spiciness.

Ingredients

- 2 ½ pounds of potatoes, peeled
- 35 ounces of water
- 1 teaspoon glucose syrup (confectioner's glucose)
- 1 tablespoon coarse salt
- 1/2 teaspoon baking soda

- 1/4 cup of grapeseed oil
- Salt, to your liking
- 1 tablespoon ancho chili powder
- 1 teaspoon smoked cayenne pepper
- 1 teaspoon ground cumin
- Guacamole, to serve

Directions

1. Set your cooker to 193 degrees F. Cut your potatoes into French fries (0.35 inches thick).

2. To make the brine, in a large-sized dish, combine the water, glucose syrup, coarse salt, and baking soda.

3. Then, divide the French fries among the sous vide pouches. Divide the brine among the pouches and vacuum seal.

4. Allow the bagged potato to sous vide for 18 minutes. Remove French fries from the pouches and pat them dry.

5. Next, drizzle French fries with the grapeseed oil. Toss them with salt, ancho chili powder, cayenne pepper, and ground cumin. Spread on a baking sheet that is lined with a parchment paper.

6. Bake in the preheated oven at 350 degrees F for 20 minutes. Flip them over.

7. Turn the oven temperature to 450 degrees F. Bake for a further 10 minutes or until potatoes are just browned. Serve with guacamole.

129. THAI-STYLE VEGETABLE BITES

8 Servings

Ready in about
1 hour

PER SERVING:
140 Calories; 6.9g Fat;
17.0g Carbs; 2.4g Protein;
12.0g Sugars

This Thai-style sauce adds a spicy and sharp taste to these amazing vegetables, making them less boring and more appealing! Sprinkle with toasted sesame seeds if desired.

Ingredients

- 2 cauliflower heads, broken into florets
- 1/2 pound of Vidalia onions, peeled and cut into wedges
- 4 tablespoons of peanut oil
- 1 teaspoon red pepper flakes, crushed
- Sea salt flakes and ground black pepper, to taste

For Thai-Style Sauce

- 1/2 cup of rice vinegar
- 1/2 cup of water
- 1/3 cup of sugar
- 2 garlic cloves, smashed
- 1/2 teaspoon hot sauce
- 1 teaspoon cornstarch

Directions

1. Set your cooking machine to 184 degrees F.

2. Toss cauliflower florets and onion wedges with peanut oil, red pepper flakes, salt, and black pepper. Transfer each type of vegetable to a separate sous vide pouch.

3. Lower the pouches into the preheated water bath. Allow the bagged vegetables to sous vide for 50 minutes.

4. Remove the vegetables from the pouches and pat them dry with a dish cloth.

5. Pour rice vinegar and water into a pan that is preheated over a medium-high flame; bring to a boil. Add the sugar, garlic, and hot sauce and turn the heat to a simmer; simmer for 4 to 6 minutes.

6. Take the pan off the heat and gradually add cornstarch, whisking constantly. Arrange your veggies in a serving bowl. Serve with Thai-Style sauce on the side.

130. Super Crispy Zingy Wings

8 Servings

Ready in about
2 hours 40 minutes
+ marinating time

PER SERVING:
128 Calories; 2.3g Fat;
2.9g Carbs; 22.1g Protein;
1.1g Sugars

According to a National Chicken Council report, "Americans will eat 1.33 billion chicken wings on Super Bowl Sunday". Taking into account that most of those are deep-fried and dipped in fatty sauces, wings can't be healthy. Luckily, these wings are cooked sous vide and baked in an oven with a little oil.

Ingredients

- 8 chicken wings, bone-in

For the Marinade:

- 4 sprigs of fresh thyme, chopped
- 1 teaspoon smoked paprika
- Sea salt and cracked black pepper, to your liking
- 1 Scotch bonnet chili, minced
- 1 bunch of green onions, coarsely chopped

- 1 (1-inch piece) fresh ginger, peeled and chopped
- 3 garlic cloves, coarsely chopped
- 1 ½ tablespoons of tamari sauce
- 1 tablespoon champagne vinegar
- 1 tablespoon dry white wine
- Fresh juice of 1 lime

Directions

1. Set your cooker to 165 degrees F. Pat chicken wings dry with a dish cloth

2. Then, pulse all ingredients for the marinade in your blender or a food processor. Add chicken wings and let them marinate for 2 hours.

3. Add chicken wings to sous vide bags, reserving the marinade. Allow the bagged wings to sous vide for 2 hours 30 minutes.

4. Remove the bagged chicken from the water bath. Arrange chicken wings in a single layer on a disposable aluminum foil pan or baking pan.

5. Position an oven rack in the center of the oven and preheat the broiler. Afterwards, broil the chicken wings until the skin is deeply browned and crisp, about 10 minutes.

6. Baste the wings with the reserved marinade every few minutes and flip them occasionally with tongs. Bon appétit!

131. GREEK-STYLE STUFFED GRAPE TOMATOES

10 Servings

Ready in about
24 hours

PER SERVING:
218 Calories; 16.3g Fat;
3.2g Carbs; 14.2g Protein;
1.7g Sugars

Here's the recipe for one of the favorite party snacks! You can take this sous vide bacon to potlucks because it can be cooked in advance and then prepared on a grill or in a pan. Grape tomatoes are bite-sized tomatoes that are available year-round.

Ingredients

- 3/4 pounds of bacon, cut into thick slices
- 1/2 cup of Feta cheese, crumbled
- 1/4 cup of Greek yogurt
- 1 heaping tablespoon fresh parsley, chopped

- 1 teaspoon oregano
- 3 cups of grape tomatoes, cleaned and hollowed-out
- 1/4 cup of Kalamata olives, pitted and sliced

Directions

1. Set your device to 142 degrees F.

2. Allow the bagged bacon to sous vide for 24 hours. Remove the bag from the water bath; pat the bacon slices dry with paper towels.

3. Then, cook the bacon in the frying pan that is preheated over a medium-high heat for about 1 minute 30 seconds. Flip on the other side using a spatula and cook for 1 minute more.

4. Chop the bacon and transfer to a mixing bowl. Add crumbled Feta cheese, Greek yogurt, parsley, and oregano; mix to combine well.

5. Then, fill your tomatoes with the bacon stuffing. Top with sliced Kalamata olives and arrange on a serving platter. Bon appétit!

132. ROASTED ASPARAGUS WITH YOGURT SAUCE

6 Servings

Ready in about
1 hour

PER SERVING:
107 Calories; 5.1g Fat;
12.9g Carbs; 4.5g Protein;
6.8g Sugars

Cooking asparagus sous vide leads to extraordinarily tender and juicy but still crispy bites. Keep the yogurt sauce in your refrigerator until ready to serve.

Ingredients

- 1 ½ pounds of asparagus spears, tough ends removed
- 1 pound of yellow onions, chopped
- Sea salt flakes and crushed red pepper flakes, to taste

- 2 tablespoons of olive oil
- 1/2 cup of Greek-style yogurt
- 1 tablespoon fresh lime juice
- 1/4 cup of fresh cilantro, roughly chopped

Directions

1. Set your cooking machine to 183 degrees F. Add the asparagus to a large-sized cooking pouch; season with salt and red pepper.

2. Add the onion to another bag; season with salt and red pepper.

3. Place the pouches on a rack and set the timer for 30 minutes. Now, remove the bag with the onions.

4. Set the timer for an additional 15 minutes. Remove the asparagus spears from the bag.

5. Now, toss your asparagus with olive oil and arrange them on a baking sheet in a single layer. Roast the asparagus spears for 15 minutes.

6. In the meantime, make the dipping sauce by mixing the cooked onions with Greek-style yogurt, lime juice, and fresh cilantro. Serve with roasted asparagus and enjoy!

133. Two-Cheese and Shrimp Scampi Dip

10 Servings

Ready in about
45 minutes

PER SERVING:
129 Calories; 6.2g Fat;
4.1g Carbs; 13.9g Protein;
0.6g Sugars

Small-sized shrimp cooks perfectly sous vide. If you can't find Ricotta, use whatever cream cheese you've got on hand. This crowd-pleasing dip is quick enough to cook on a weeknight!

Ingredients

- 1 pound of small-sized shrimp, peeled and deveined
- 1 teaspoon seasoned salt
- 1/4 teaspoon red pepper flakes, crushed
- 1/4 teaspoon paprika
- 2 tablespoons of lemon juice, freshly squeezed
- 2-3 bay leaves
- 4 garlic cloves, peeled and smashed
- 8 ounces of Ricotta cheese, at room temperature
- 3/4 cups of mozzarella cheese, shredded
- 4 tablespoons of mayonnaise
- 1/4 cup of sour cream
- 2 heaping tablespoons of fresh cilantro leaves, roughly chopped

Directions

1. Set your cooking machine to 135 degrees F. Season your shrimp with salt, red pepper, and paprika; drizzle with lemon juice.

2. Place in sous vide bags in a single layer; add a bay leaf to each bag. Divide the garlic among sous vide bags.

3. Once the water reaches the target temperature, lower the bag into the water bath. Allow the bagged shrimp to sous vide for 30 minutes; transfer to a cutting board. Now, chop the shrimp and transfer to a lightly greased baking dish.

4. Stir in Ricotta cheese, 1/2 cup of mozzarella, mayonnaise, and sour cream. Stir until everything is well incorporated. Top with remaining mozzarella.

5. Bake in the preheated oven at 355 degrees F for about 10 minutes. Scatter chopped cilantro over the top.

6. Serve with crackers and veggie sticks. Bon appétit!

134. Cheesy Canadian Bacon Nachos

6 Servings

Ready in about
11 hours 20 minutes

PER SERVING:
205 Calories; 9.6g Fat;
13.5g Carbs; 15.9g
Protein; 1.1g Sugars

Here's a great idea for a summer gathering! Cooking Canadian bacon sous vide leads to extraordinary results. Other topping suggestions include sour cream, chopped sweet peppers, salsa, sliced olives, and so on.

Ingredients

- 10 slices of Canadian bacon
- 1 pound of potatoes, peeled
- Salt and paprika, to taste

- 1 cup of Monterrey Jack, shredded
- 3 green onions, chopped
- 1 tablespoon sliced pickled jalapeños

Directions

1. Set your cooker to 143 degrees F.

2. Lower bagged Canadian bacon into the preheated water bath; allow it to sous vide for at least 10 hours.

3. Transfer Canadian bacon to a cutting board; chop the bacon and reserve.

4. Cut potatoes into thick slices; add them to a bowl with icy cold water to rinse away excess starches. Season potato slices with salt and smoked paprika. Transfer them to a large-sized vacuum seal bag.

5. Turn the cooker to 183 degrees F. Submerge bagged potatoes in the water bath and cook for 1 hour 15 minutes.

6. Meanwhile, mix the cheese, green onions, and sliced jalapeños in a bowl. Add chopped Canadian bacon and stir well.

7. Arrange the potato slices on a cookie sheet that is lined with parchment paper; top with cheese/bacon mixture. Bake in the preheated oven at 425 degrees F for 5 minutes or until Monterrey Jack has melted. Serve right away!

135. Jerk Ginger Pork Bites

6 Servings

Ready in about
12 hours 5 minutes
+ marinating time

PER SERVING:
225 Calories; 7.3g Fat;
17.1g Carbs; 22.0g
Protein; 16.3g Sugars

These pork bites are not only tasty but super juicy and tender! This recipe calls for the homemade sauce but you can purchase a bottle of your favorite BBQ sauce if desired. You can also spice things up and add your favorite hot sauce. The possibilities are endless!

Ingredients

- 1 pound of pork loin roast, cut into 1-inch cubes
- 1/2 teaspoon dried chili flakes
- 1/2 teaspoon seasoned salt
- 1/4 teaspoon freshly ground black pepper
- 1/4 teaspoon ground allspice
- 1 (2-inch) piece of fresh ginger, peeled and grated
- 1/2 cup of ketchup
- 1/2 cup of brown sugar

- 2 tablespoons of cider vinegar
- 2 tablespoons of water
- 1 teaspoon whole-grain mustard
- 1 teaspoon salt
- 1/2 teaspoon red pepper flakes, crushed
- 1 teaspoon garlic powder
- 1/2 teaspoon cumin powder
- Toasted sesame seeds, for garnish
- Cocktail sticks, to serve

Directions

1. Set your cooker to 176 degrees F. Season pork cubes with chili flakes, salt, black pepper, and ground allspice; add grated fresh ginger. Let them marinate for at least 3 hours.

2. Transfer marinated pork cubes to a sous vide pouch and vacuum seal; allow the bagged pork to sous vide for 12 hours. Pat the pork cubes dry using a dish cloth.

3. In a mixing dish, prepare the sauce by mixing ketchup, sugar, cider vinegar, water, mustard, salt, red pepper, garlic powder, and cumin powder.

4. Next step, preheat your oven to 395 degrees. Toss pork chunks with the prepared sauce and arrange them on a baking sheet.

5. Bake for 4 to 5 minutes and sprinkle warm pork cubes with toasted sesame. Finally, add cocktail sticks and enjoy your party!

136. MAPLE-GLAZED ROOT VEGETABLES

6 Servings

Ready in about
1 hour 30 minutes

PER SERVING:
169 Calories; 5.0g Fat;
30.8g Carbs; 2.2g Protein;
13.9g Sugars

You'll wow your family and guests with these sticky and succulent vegetable bites.
Serve with a sparkling wine as an aperitif.

Ingredients

- 2 golden beets, peeled and sliced 1/2-inch thick
- 5 carrots, peeled and cut diagonally into sticks
- 3 parsnips, peeled and cut diagonally into sticks
- 2 tablespoons of pure maple syrup

- 1 teaspoon peanut oil
- 1 tablespoon fresh or dried basil
- 2 tablespoons of unsalted butter
- Salt and ground black pepper, to taste
- 3 teaspoons of champagne vinegar

Directions

1. Set your cooking machine to 183 degrees F.

2. Then, place each type of vegetable in a separate cooking pouch; place the pouches on a rack.

3. Set the timer for 1 hour; when the cooking is complete, remove the vegetables from the pouches.

4. Toss the vegetables with the remaining ingredients.

5. Arrange the vegetables on two sturdy rimmed baking sheets. Cover with aluminum foil and roast for 30 minutes.

137. ARTICHOKES WITH GARLIC-BUTTER DIP

6 Servings

Ready in about
2 hours 20 minutes

PER SERVING:
214 Calories; 15.6g Fat;
17.5g Carbs; 5.6g Protein;
1.7g Sugars

Artichokes are packed with vitamins, antioxidants, and dietary fiber. Butter dips with garlic are a classic and they go well with this impressive vegetable! You can make even better dip by adding your favorite fresh aromatics.

Ingredients

- 6 artichokes, rinsed
- Juice of 1 fresh lemon
- 1 teaspoon celery salt
- 1 teaspoon red pepper flakes, crushed
- 1 stick of butter, melted

- 1 tablespoon fresh basil
- 1 tablespoon fresh parsley, minced
- 1 garlic clove, minced
- 1 tablespoon of fresh lemon juice

Directions

1. Set your cooker to 192 degrees F.

2. Cut about 1 inch from the top of each artichoke.

3. Then, rub the cut portion of the artichoke with the fresh lemon juice. Also, cut off the thorn tips of the petals with kitchen scissors. Season them with celery salt and red pepper.

4. Place your artichokes in two large-sized cooking pouches. Vacuum seal and cook for 2 hours 10 minutes. Pat them dry with a dish cloth.

5. Meanwhile, make the dipping sauce by whisking the other ingredients. Keep in your fridge until ready to serve.

6. Preheat your grill to high. Grill lightly the greased artichokes for 3 to 4 minutes; using tongs, flip on the other side and cook an additional 3 to 4 minutes.

7. Serve with the garlic-butter sauce on the side. Bon appétit!

138. Mashed Potato-Onion Balls

6 Servings

Ready in about
1 hour 15 minutes

PER SERVING:
203 Calories; 13.2g Fat;
14.7g Carbs; 7.4g Protein;
1.9g Sugars

You can make these balls for Thanksgiving feast instead of classic mashed potatoes and amaze your guests. Once cooked, the mashed potatoes can also be returned to their cooking pouches and kept hot for up to 2 hours at 140 degrees F until ready to use. You can double or triple the recipe.

Ingredients

- 1 pound of Russet potatoes, peeled and diced
- 1 yellow onion, peeled and diced
- 1 teaspoon red pepper flakes, crushed
- Salt and black pepper, to taste
- 1 teaspoon garlic powder

- 3 tablespoons of mozzarella cheese, shredded
- 2 eggs
- 1 cup of seasoned breadcrumbs
- 1 cup of canola oil, for frying

Directions

1. Set your cooker to 183 degrees F. Place the diced potatoes in a large-sized sous vide bag. Place the onions in another sous vide bag.

2. Place the bags on a rack. Set the timer for 30 minutes. Then, transfer the bag of onions from the water bath to a cutting board. Now, chop the onions and reserve.

3. Set the timer for another 40 minutes. After that, remove the bags of potatoes. Then, mash the potatoes together with chopped onions, red pepper flakes, salt, black pepper, and garlic powder.

4. Add mozzarella cheese and stir until everything is well incorporated.

5. Next, shape the mixture into the balls. Beat the eggs in a shallow bowl; throw the breadcrumbs into another bowl.

6. Dip the balls in the beaten eggs; then, roll them over the breadcrumbs. Cook in hot canola oil for about 5 minutes; turning periodically. Serve with cocktail sticks.

 Sous Vide Cookbook | Snacks & Appetizers

139. Exotic Za'atar Cauliflower Bites

4 Servings

Ready in about
45 minutes

PER SERVING:
108 Calories; 8.8g Fat;
6.8g Carbs; 2.5g Protein;
2.8g Sugars

Za'atar is the Middle Eastern spice blend that goes well with nature's finest products like cauliflower. You can serve these cauliflower bites with cheese cubes on a stick at your next wine party!

Ingredients

- 1 pound of cauliflower florets
- Salt and black pepper, to your liking
- 3 tablespoons of melted butter
- 3 garlic cloves, minced
- 1 tablespoon Za'atar
- 1 teaspoon hot paprika
- 1 tablespoon of sherry vinegar

Directions

1. Set your cooker to 183 degrees F. Place cauliflower florets in a large-sized cooking pouch. Season with salt and black pepper.

2. Allow the bagged cauliflower to cook for 40 minutes; then, remove the cauliflower florets from the bag and pat them dry with a paper towel.

3. In a heavy skillet that is preheated over a moderate heat, warm the butter. Once hot, stir in the garlic, Za'atar, hot paprika and sherry vinegar and cook until just aromatic; make sure to stir continuously.

4. After that, throw in the cauliflower florets and cook for a few minutes longer or until thoroughly heated. Serve with toothpicks.

140. KALE CHIPS WITH OLD-FASHIONED SALSA

8 Servings

Ready in about
1 hour 10 minutes

PER SERVING:
164 Calories; 9.6g Fat;
19.5g Carbs; 4.0g Protein;
3.5g Sugars

Salsa is usually accompanied by tortilla chips or crackers. This recipe
calls for healthy and low-calorie kale chips. If your mouths are already watering,
give this recipe a try!

Ingredients

For the Salsa:

- 3 ears of corn, shucked
- 1 teaspoon red pepper flakes, crushed
- 1 teaspoon kosher salt
- 1/2 cup of green bell pepper, chopped
- 2 garlic cloves, peeled and minced
- 1 cup of onion, diced
- 1 jalapeño, finely chopped
- 1 cup of tomatoes, chopped
- 2 ½ tablespoons of fresh lime juice

- 3 tablespoons of olive oil
- 1/4 cup of fresh cilantro, minced

For the Kale Chips:

- 1 bunch of kale, rinsed and
- 2 tablespoons of extra-virgin olive oil
- 1/2 teaspoon garlic powder
- 1 teaspoon shallot powder
- 1/3 teaspoon smoked paprika
- Himalayan sea salt, to taste

Directions

1. Set your cooking machine to 182 degrees F.

2. Sprinkle the corn with red pepper flakes and salt. Place the corn in a sous vide pouch and vacuum seal.

3. Allow the bagged corn to sous vide for 40 minutes.

4. While the corn is cooking, thoroughly mix the other ingredients for the salsa. Now, cut the kernels away from the cobs; add them to the salsa mix and stir well.

5. Next, tear the kale leaves up into large-sized pieces.

6. Toss the kale with the remaining ingredients and transfer to a baking sheet that is lined with parchment paper.

7. Bake in a single layer for 10 minutes; now, rotate the baking sheet and bake for another 12 minutes. Serve with prepared salsa. Bon appétit!

DESSERTS

141

144

146

148

150

141. Crema Catalana with Raspberries

8 Servings

Ready in about
2 hours 45 minutes
+ chilling time

PER SERVING:
420 Calories; 31.3g Fat;
33.1g Carbs; 4.8g Protein;
29.0g Sugars

> Add fresh raspberries on the top and make your dessert a little more excessive.
> If you don't want to heat up the oven, use a mini blowtorch or a grill
> to caramelize the sugar.

Ingredients

- 3 ½ cups of heavy cream
- A big slice of a peel from an orange
- 1 vanilla pod, split and seeds reserved
- 3/4 cups of caster sugar

- 7 egg yolks
- 1 teaspoon ground anise
- 2 tablespoons of brown sugar
- 1 cup of fresh raspberries, washed

Directions

1. In a saucepan, heat the heavy cream, bringing to a gentle boil (to about 150 degrees F).

2. Now, stir in the peel from an orange and 1 vanilla pod; allow the flavors to blend for 1 hour 30 minutes.

3. Next, bring the heavy cream up to 175 degrees F.

4. Set your cooker to 183 degrees F. Whisk the caster sugar, egg yolks, and ground anise until the sugar has dissolved. Now, gradually add the hot heavy cream, whisking continuously until everything's well incorporated.

5. Place the mixture in a large-sized cooking pouch; vacuum seal. Lower the cooking pouch into the preheated water bath and cook for 1 hour 10 minutes.

6. Transfer the custard mixture to individual dishes; cover and place in your refrigerator for 24 hours.

7. Before serving, sprinkle the top of each individual cream with brown sugar; place the dishes under the broiler until sugar melts, approximately 2 minutes. Serve right away garnished with fresh raspberries. Bon appétit!

142. CURD DE CLÉMENTINE WITH BERRIES

8 Servings

Ready in about
1 hour
+ chilling time

PER SERVING:
219 Calories; 14.6g Fat;
19.2g Carbs; 5.0g Protein;
14.0g Sugars

Desserts don't have to be complicated to impress your guests. This is a versatile recipe; you can serve this curd on top of meringue cookies or pancakes. It couldn't be easier!

Ingredients

- 5 clementines, finely grated zest and juiced
- 12 ounces of sugar
- A pinch of salt
- 5 eggs

- 1 stick of butter, cubed
- 1 cup of blueberries
- 1 cup of strawberries
- 8 teaspoons of graham cracker crumbs

Directions

1. Set your cooker to 182 degrees F.

2. Mix the zest and the juice of the clementines with the sugar, a pinch of salt, eggs, and butter in your blender or a food processor.

3. Transfer the curd mixture to a large sous vide bag and vacuum seal. Submerge the bag in the preheated water; allow the bagged mixture to sous vide for 1 hour.

4. Spoon the curd into a bowl. Cover the bowl with a plastic wrap, and chill completely in your refrigerator.

5. Then, alternate layers of curd and berries in eight dessert bowls. Top each serving with crumbs and serve well chilled.

143. Creamy Chocolate Dream Dessert

4 Servings

Ready in about
45 minutes
+ chilling time

PER SERVING:
452 Calories; 31.6g Fat;
35.3g Carbs; 8.6g Protein;
29.7g Sugars

This is a family all-time favorite dessert! The great thing about this recipe is that any variety of chocolate will work. Delectable!

Ingredients

- 1 ¼ cups of heavy cream
- 1/2 cup of milk
- 1 cup of milk chocolate
- 1 ½ tablespoons of honey
- 1 whole egg
- 3 egg yolks

- 1/4 teaspoon cinnamon powder
- 1 tablespoon cocoa powder
- 1/2 teaspoon pure almond extract
- A pinch of kosher salt
- A pinch of freshly grated nutmeg

Directions

1. Set the cooker to 182 degrees F. Add the water according to recommended minimum water level.

2. In a pan, warm the heavy whipping cream and milk. Now, add the chocolate and honey; allow to rest for 4 for 6 minutes.

3. In the meantime, beat the eggs with cinnamon powder, cocoa powder, almond extract, salt, and nutmeg. Add to the cream mixture.

4. Fill the jars with the mixture and close their lids; put the jars into the hot water bath and cook for 35 minutes.

5. Next, remove the jars from the water bath and allow them to cool to room temperature; then, chill in your refrigerator.

6. Garnish with ice cream and enjoy!

144. CHOCOLATE-DIPPED FRUIT KABOBS

8 Servings

Ready in about
20 minutes
+ chilling time

PER SERVING:
280 Calories; 14.8g Fat;
33.4g Carbs; 3.9g Protein;
28.5g Sugars

The homemade chocolate sauce is very customizable and easy to make at home! You can enjoy this silky and sophisticated dessert all year long, adding seasonal fruit combinations.

Ingredients

- 14 ounces of chocolate chunks
- A pinch of salt
- 1/4 teaspoon freshly grated nutmeg

- 1 pound of fresh fruits (apple, banana, kiwifruit, oranges), bite-sized
- A few wooden skewers

Directions

1. Set your cooker to 120 degrees F.

2. Lay the chocolate, salt, and grated nutmeg into a sous vide bag. Allow the bagged chocolate to sous vide for 12 minutes.

3. Turn the temperature to 90 degrees F. Continue cooking for 5 more minutes, making sure that the chocolate is fully melted.

4. Dip each piece of fruit in the chocolate. Transfer to a tray lined with wax paper. Allow them to chill in the refrigerator for about 1 hour.

5. Thread the fruit on wooden skewers and arrange on a serving platter. Bon appétit!

145. KID-FRIENDLY CHOCOLATE CHEESECAKE IN A JAR

8 Servings

Ready in about
1 hour 25 minutes
+ chilling time

PER SERVING:
354 Calories; 25.8g Fat;
27.9g Carbs; 4.9g Protein;
22.5g Sugars

This chocolate cheesecake is an impressive dessert that is extra easy to make using sous vide technique. Once you taste how good this cheesecake is, it will become a staple during the summer season.

Ingredients

- 1 ½ cups of cream cheese, softened
- 1/4 cup of sour cream
- 1/3 cup of sugar
- 2 eggs
- A pinch of salt
- A pinch of ground anise star
- 1 cup of semisweet chocolate chips

Directions

1. Set your cooker to 175 degrees F.

2. In a mixing dish, thoroughly combine the cream cheese, sour cream, and sugar until well mixed.

3. Add the eggs, salt, and anise star; mix until well beaten. Fold in the chocolate and mix on low speed until well-blended. Spoon the mixture into the jars.

4. Cover your jars with the lids and allow them to sous vide for 1 hour 25 minutes. Remove the jars from the water bath and allow them to cool completely.

5. Just before serving, garnish with whipped cream and serve well chilled. Bon appétit!

146. Sweet Risotto with Apricots and Figs

4 Servings

Ready in about
2 hours 10 minutes

PER SERVING:
334 Calories; 5.9g Fat;
64.0g Carbs; 8.4g Protein;
22.3g Sugars

There are a zillion creative ideas for sweet risotto; thus, get inspired by this delectable sous vide dessert and create your unique combo of spices and fruits. Keep this recipe in your back pocket!

Ingredients

- 2 cups of milk
- 1 cup of jasmine rice
- 1 tablespoon coconut oil
- 4 tablespoons of agave nectar
- 5-6 dried figs, chopped
- 3-4 dried apricots, chopped
- 1/2 teaspoon vanilla paste
- 1 teaspoon ground cinnamon

Directions

1. Set your cooking device to 140 degrees F.

2. Then, place all of the above ingredients into a sous vide bag; shake to distribute evenly and vacuum seal.

3. Allow it to sous vide for 2 hours 10 minutes.

4. Serve at room temperature in individual bowls and enjoy!

147. POACHED PEACHES IN VANILLA WINE SYRUP

4 Servings

Ready in about
40 minutes

PER SERVING:
142 Calories; 3.3g Fat;
26.6g Carbs; 1.4g Protein;
26.1g Sugars

These simple and totally decadent poached peaches are a must-have for Sunday afternoon! The cassia buds are available in specialty-food stores and you can order them online as well. It has floral, cinnamon taste, which makes it perfect addition for poached fruits.

Ingredients

- 4 tablespoons of caster sugar
- 3 teaspoons butter, unsalted
- 2 tablespoons of fresh lime juice
- 1/4 cup of dry white wine
- 1 vanilla bean, seeds scraped
- 4 firm peaches, pitted and halved lengthwise

- 4 cassia buds, crushed
- 2 whole cloves
- 1/2 teaspoon of allspice berries, coarsely crushed
- 1 heaping tablespoon fresh mint leaves

Directions

1. Set your cooker to 183 degrees F.

2. To make the sauce, warm the sugar, butter, lime juice, wine, and vanilla seeds over a moderate heat. Stir continuously until just thickened.

3. Add the peaches to a sous vide bag. Now, add the cassia buds, whole cloves, and allspice berries; vacuum seal.

4. Lower the bagged peaches into the preheated water bath; cook for 40 minutes.

5. Serve peaches on individual plates; spoon the sauce over them and serve garnished with fresh mint leaves. Bon appétit!

148. DELECTABLE GINGERSNAP PUMPKIN PIE

10 Servings

Ready in about
1 hour 35 minutes
+ chilling time

PER SERVING:
274 Calories; 14.6g Fat;
32.3g Carbs; 5.5g Protein;
24.5g Sugars

There are so many ways to make pumpkin pie. This light-as-air pumpkin pie is perfect for any occasion. Serve well chilled.

Ingredients

- 1 ¼ cups of brown sugar
- 2 ¼ cups of canned pumpkin
- 5 large eggs
- 1 cup of whipped cream
- 1 cup of milk

- 1 ½ teaspoons of pumpkin pie spice blend
- A pinch of kosher salt
- 1 ¼ cups of gingersnap cookie crumbs
- 5 tablespoons of unsalted butter, softened
- 3 tablespoons of sugar

Directions

1. Set your cooking machine to 175 degrees F.

2. Then, puree brown sugar with canned pumpkin and eggs in your food processor; puree until everything is well incorporated.

3. Then, mix in the whipped cream, milk, pumpkin pie spice blend, and salt; mix well.

4. Next, transfer the mixture to a large-sized sous vide bag. Vacuum seal and lower into the preheated water bath. Allow it to sous vide for 1 hour 20 minutes.

5. In the meantime, make the crust by mixing the remaining ingredients in your food processor.

6. Press the crust mixture into a pie plate. Bake the crust in the preheated oven at 325 degrees F for about 15 minutes; allow it to cool completely.

7. Remove the bag from the water bath and let it cool slightly. Spread the pumpkin mixture onto the prepared crust. Place your pie in the refrigerator for 10 hours.

8. To serve, top with whipped cream and garnish with crushed gingersnap cookies. Bon appétit!

149. Holiday Dulce de Leche Pudding

6 Servings

Ready in about
14 hours 45 minutes

PER SERVING:
361 Calories; 14.3g
Fat; 43.6g Carbs; 13.0g
Protein; 8.6g Sugars

This unconventional combo of sophisticated Dulce de Leche, sweet raisin and dark rum makes this gooey and rich pudding that can satisfy the most intense sweet tooth!

Ingredients

- 1/2 (14-ounce) can of condensed milk, sweetened
- Seeds of 1/2 vanilla bean
- 1/4 teaspoon table salt
- 1/2 stick of butter, melted
- 2 whole eggs

- 3 egg whites
- 1 cup of whole milk
- 1 tablespoon dark rum
- 1 pound of sweet raisin bread, torn into chunks

Directions

1. Set your cooker to 183 degrees F.

2. Add the condensed milk, vanilla and salt to a large-sized sous vide bag; vacuum seal. Then, submerge the bag in the preheated water bath and cook for 14 hours 30 minutes.

3. Remove your Dulce de Leche from the bag and allow it to cool slightly.

4. Then, cream the butter with eggs and egg whites. Add the milk and dark rum; beat again. Add the prepared Dulce de Leche.

5. Afterwards, throw in the bread chunks and mix until everything is well combined.

6. Spoon the mixture into a lightly greased baking pan. Bake in the preheated oven at 425 degrees F for about 15 minutes, rotating the pan once or twice. Bon appétit!

150. Mint Chocolate Lover's Dream

10 Servings

Ready in about
3 hours
+ chilling time

PER SERVING:
331 Calories; 17.6g Fat;
39.8g Carbs; 4.4g Protein;
26.0g Sugars

These jar cookies are so cheap but better than many expensive cookies you've ever had. Refreshing minty flavor in combination with delightful chocolate is every dessert lover's dream!

Ingredients

- 1 tablespoon of butter, for greasing
- 1 ¼ cups of all-purpose white flour
- 1/2 teaspoon baking soda
- 1 teaspoon baking powder
- 1 stick of butter, softened
- 3/4 cups of caster sugar

- 2 whole eggs
- Seeds from 1 vanilla pod
- 1/4 teaspoon ground anise star
- 1 teaspoon peppermint extract
- 1 ¼ cups of chocolate chunks
- 15 thin chocolate mints, crushed

Directions

1. Set the cooker to 193 degrees F. Butter the bottom and sides of 5 canning jars and set them aside.

2. In a mixing dish, thoroughly combine the flour, baking soda, and baking powder, and salt.

3. Then, cream the butter with sugar using an electric mixer; mix until fluffy. Fold in the eggs, one at a time, and continue beating until well mixed and pale.

4. Add the flour mixture to the butter mixture; throw in the vanilla seeds, anise star, and peppermint extract; mix to combine well.

5. Fold in the chocolate chunks and crushed mints; mix again. Spoon the batter into the greased jars. Now, seal the jars and transfer them to the preheated water bath; allow them to sous vide for 2 hours 40 minutes.

6. Remove the jars from the water bath and let them cool completely. Then, remove the cookie mixture from the jars and chill in your refrigerator for 2 hours.

7. Lastly, slice your cookies into the desired size and arrange on a serving platter. Bon appétit!

Made in the USA
Middletown, DE
08 November 2018